MUSIC ON THE BORDERLAND

MUSIC ON THE BORDERLAND

Remembering and Chronicling the 1979 Revolution's Shadow on Iranian Music

Keyan Emami

Condensed from University of Toronto Doctoral Research (2020)

ASEMANA BOOKS

Toronto, Canada

FIRST EDITION

Copyright © 2024 by Asemana Books

ALL RIGHTS RESERVED.

No part of this book may be reproduced or transmitted in any form or by any means, electronic or mechanical, including photocopying, recording, or by any information storage and retrieval system, without prior written permission from the publisher, except for the inclusion of brief quotations in a review.

Published by ASEMANA BOOKS

ISBN: 978-1-7382855-5-6

Book Design: Asemana Books

Cover Art: Asemana Books

To find out more about our authors and books visit:

www.asemanabooks.ca

ASEMANA
BOOKS

In loving memory of my father,

In gratitude to my parents,

always.

Contents

About the Author xi
Words of Thanks xiii
Note on Transliteration xv

Prelude: A Letter to My Father 17
Overture: Iranian Music Post-Revolution 19
Methodology 23

Part I: Macro Perspectives 25
Revolutionary Echoes: Previous Generation Narratives 27
    Media and Music (1979–1989) 27
    The Rise of Artwashing and Censorship 42

Part II: Micro Perspectives 59
Keyan's Journey: A Musical Odyssey 61
    1. Revelation: The Wind of Change 62
    2. Harmony: The Sound of Music 63
    3. Turmoil: The War (1980–1988) 65
    4. Uncertainty: Postwar Music Education 71
    5. Dissonance: Lost 74
    6. Quest: In Search of Lost Time 84
    7. Solidarity: A Composer's Tribute to Loss 86

Coda: Post-Revolution Music 89
Postlude: A Celebration of Rebirth 93
Epilogue 95

Appendices 97
Glossary 109
References 115

About the Author

Keyan Emami, a Juno-nominated composer, is celebrated for his contemporary works inspired by Persian literature and various musical forms. Renowned for his orchestral, vocal, and piano compositions, his music has garnered international recognition, acclaimed as "eloquent and poignant" and "dark and moving."

As the co-founder and artistic director of Key Music Productions and the ICOT collective, Emami brings a wealth of expertise to his compositions, drawing from his doctoral studies in composition at the University of Toronto. Alongside his illustrious career as a composer, Emami serves as an RCM Certified Music Teacher and Adjudicator at The Royal Conservatory College of Examiners, enriching the next generation of musicians with his passion and knowledge.

Emami's monograph, *Music on the Borderland*, offers readers a captivating exploration of the complex and evolving landscape of Iranian music. Through meticulous research and personal insight, Emami invites readers to delve into the untold stories and creative journeys of Iranian composers, shedding light on the diverse influences that shape their artistic expression. This monograph marks the first part of a trilogy about Emami's lived experiences.

Furthermore, Emami has composed two additional musical works as part of this trilogy: "Journey Inwards," an orchestral exploration reflecting the composer's inner psychological reality, and "The Black Fish," a musical interpretation of imaginative landscapes evoking strong emotions. Together, they offer a profound journey through themes of identity, resilience, and artistic expression. Explore more at www.keyanemami.com.

Words of Thanks

I extend my deepest gratitude to my mother, Dr. Fakhri Sheikholeslami, for her unconditional support and faith in me. Your encouragement has meant the world to me. I also thank my sister, Kataneh Emami for taking the time out of her busy schedule to provide her thoughts and comments.

I am thankful to all my family, friends, and colleagues who have provided me with tremendous intellectual and emotional support from the outset of this project: Kate Tavasoli, Vahid Mansoori, Zahra Mansoori, Mehdi Farahani, Navid Bargrizan, Joanna Warden, Nima Sadat-Tehrani, Shahin Fayaz, Khashayar Bavarasad, Rana Mireskandari, Ali Abbasi, Aryo Nazaradeh, Shohreh Shaghaghian, Nil Basdurak, Hamidreza Salehyar, Hadi Milanloo, and Mahdi Ganjavi.

I also extend my appreciation to all my teachers who have guided me through my journey: Ahmad Pejman, Alexander Rapoport, Chan Ka Nin, Christos Hatzis, Eliot Britton, Farid Omran, Farman Behboud, Farzaneh Hemmasi, Gabriel Prokofiev, Gary Kulesha, Hamidreza Dibazar, Hossein Dehlavi, James Kippen, Kambiz Roshanravan, Khayyam Mirzazade, Mark Sallmen, Mehran Rouhani, Michael Colgrass, Michael Patrick Albano, Mostafa Kamal Pourtorab, Nasim Niknafs, Norbert Palej, Paul Chihara, Robert Rival, Ryan McClelland, Sebastiano Bisciglia, Sharif Lotfi, Steven Mackey, Steven Vande Moortele, and Tolib Shahidi.

Note on Transliteration

In this book, the transliteration of Persian terms follows a simplified approach to facilitate readability for a broad audience. Diacritical marks have been minimized to avoid confusion, but essential ones, such as the macron (ā), are mainly retained to distinguish long vowels. For instance, "Chādor" is used instead of more complex transliterations. The macron (ā) represents the long "a" sound in Persian 'ا'. Additionally, the letter "x" is used to represent the Persian letter 'خ', while "q" is used for both 'ق' and 'غ', as seen in terms like "Barpāxiz" and "qad-e qan." While "q" and "x" are frequently used for 'ق' and 'خ' in this book, note that "gh" and "kh" may also be used in some instances, as in the cases of "Ghotbzadeh" and "Khomeini." This decision may vary depending on personal preference or specific linguistic considerations. This is especially true for specific names (proper nouns) like the names of individuals or recognized entities. Furthermore, please note that the letter 'ش' is transliterated as "sh" in some instances, and as "š" or "ś" in others, depending on the linguistic context.

Terms are transliterated to reflect their phonetic pronunciation in Persian as closely as possible while also being mindful of common English spelling conventions. This approach strikes a balance between linguistic accuracy and reader accessibility. For some terms, the transliteration is based on colloquial pronunciation instead of the written pronunciation to ensure smoother readability. For example, "Sedā o Simā" is used instead of "Sedā va Simā." Consistency in transliteration is maintained throughout the text to ensure clarity.

Prelude: A Letter to My Father

Bābā! Why do we live in an old modest apartment while your lower-ranked officers live in the most luxurious mansions and penthouses in the northern district of Tehran?[1] *Bābā*, why did we drive the same second-hand car for over twenty years while your subordinates, not nearly as educated or as competent as you, purchased brand new cars almost every year? *Bābā*, why didn't you continue working in the army as a major-general after the revolution—were you a coward? Why didn't you raise me to be an *Āqāzādeh*—were you short-sighted?[2] Why didn't you stay in the Iranian army after the 1979 Revolution to defend Iran during the war—were you a traitor? *Bābā*, why did you instead play the violin several hours every day—repeating the same étude again and again and again—during a time when five hundred thousand soldiers died? Were you rehearsing for a recital that never happened?

Bābā, I do not recollect what other questions I asked you throughout all those years. However, I remember that you never talked much about your past, especially about the couple of years after 1979. Your personal trauma led to your heart attack in 1980. You endeavored to overcome the traumatic stress of the revolution by pouring yourself into music and sports.

---

[1] *Bābā* means 'dad' in Persian.
[2] *Āqāzādeh* is a term that entered colloquialism in Iran in the 1990s to describe the children of the political or ruling elite who emerge as the men of means and influence, usually in a way that reflects familial nepotism and corruption.

Thirty years later, I fathomed all your silent pain and restrained suffering on Monday, June 8, 2009—the day we received the result of your CAT scans and we were informed that you suffered from dementia. Perhaps the last resort was to forget. However, you never asked me to forget our past. Today, I believe that the best way to heal is to tell our story.

Overture: Exploring Iranian Music and Composers in the Wake of the Revolution

هنوز ما را «اهلیّت گفت» نیست،
کاشکی «اهلیّت شنودن» بودی.
«تمام ـ گفتن» می‌باید و «تمام ـ شنودن»!

بر دل‌ها مُهر است،
بر زبان‌ها مُهر است،
و بر گوش‌ها مُهر است.

شمس تبریزی، آیاتِ شمس (شماره ۱۶۷)

We are not yet "docile to speak",
Wish we were "docile to hear."
A must it is "to say it all" and "to hear it all"!

Hearts sealed,
Tongues sealed,
And ears sealed.

Shams Tabrizi, Āyāt [Verses] (*No. 167*)[3]

---

[3] Shams Tabrizi (1185-1248) was a poet, sufi and spiritual instructor of Rumi.

This study sheds light on the sociopolitical context of music in Iran from the 1979 Revolution to 1989 and the stories of contemporary Iranian composers who have studied music, have worked as professional musicians and have composed music. It outlines their social challenges, and how they have overcome them. The focus is particularly on their personal, educational, and professional stories and experiences. In addition, this book demonstrates the events that inspired them, and the pivotal points in their developmental path that transformed them.

Despite several obstacles, strict regulations, and vague guidelines imposed by the Iranian government, contemporary composers have continued their musical activities in Iran and abroad. Notwithstanding all adversities, resilient composers flourished, created new works, and rose from the ashes—like a phoenix.

The rationale for conducting this research is threefold: First, as an Iranian-Canadian composer whose education, career, and life have been extensively impacted by the history of the past decades in Iran, I intend to discover and narrate the stories of contemporary Iranian composers, and compare them with my personal life story. Second, a remarkable increase in the number of Iranian music students at the University of Toronto and other Canadian universities has occurred over the past twenty years. This study can serve as a source of information on the influence of the 1979 Revolution and the

Iran-Iraq war on contemporary Iranian-born composers.[4] Hence, it benefits a wide spectrum of audiences including, but not limited to, Iranian students, other international students, and their instructors at the Canadian universities. Third, even though considerable literature exists that describes the history and different aspects of music in Iran after the 1979 Revolution, scholars have not conducted in-depth research projects on how the chain of events affected contemporary Iranian composers' perspectives, life-changing decisions, and creative outputs.[5]

The main question that the research aspires to answer is whether and how major events during the revolution, war and post-war eras have affected the professional and personal lives of Iranian-born composers and their works in general, and how they have leveraged their capabilities and opportunities to face and overcome hindrances.

---

[4] The Iran-Iraq War, lasting from 1980 to 1988, was a devasting conflict that profoundly impacted Iran's socio-political landscape, cultural development, and economy.

[5] See for example Breyley, 2016; Breyley & Fatemi, 2016; Hemmasi, 2020; Niknafs, 2016; Nooshin, 2005, 2017; Randall, 2004; Semati, 2017; Seyedsayamdost, 2017; Shahshahani, 2013; Youssefzadeh, 2000.

Methodology

This project employs qualitative methods, including the analysis of interviews from various documentaries and autoethnography. It utilizes the narratives of contemporary Iranian composers, officials, and other music-related professionals in documentary films, as well as my own autoethnography, to portray the impact of Iran's sociopolitical climate on Iranian composers after the 1979 Revolution. According to Creswell (2012), "It is typical in qualitative research to study a few individuals. This is because the overall ability of a researcher to provide an in-depth picture diminishes with the addition of each new individual" (p. 209). He continues, "In homogeneous sampling, the researcher purposefully samples individuals based on membership in a subgroup that has defining characteristics. To use this procedure, the researcher needs to identify the characteristics and find individuals that possess them" (p. 208). This research illuminates and explores the experiences of contemporary, middle-class, Iranian-born composers, with similar cultural backgrounds. According to Seidman (2006), individual behavior becomes meaningful and understandable when placed within the context in which it occurs. Thus, studying personal thoughts and experiences within the context of the existing circumstances provides individuals with the opportunity to reflect on the underlying reasons and motives for their decisions. As Seidman further argues, it is important for researchers to identify the autobiographical roots of their interest in their topic of study. This project describes my narratives, including excerpts of major life events to further clarify and address the purpose of this research. Through sketching personal memories and pondering how circumstances impacted each experience, I selected and described some of these highlights comprehensively.

PART I:

Macro Perspectives

Echoes of the Revolution: Narratives From the Previous Generation

The 1979 Revolution, Media, and Music (1979–1989)

»گفتا: ز که نالیم؟ که از ماست که بر ماست«

ناصر خسرو، قصیدۀ شماره ٤٤

Lest we whimper! As you sow, so shall you reap.
Naser Khosrow, Ode no. 44[6]

The Merriam-Webster Dictionary defines "Revolution" as "a sudden, complete, radical change," which is exactly what happened in Iran right after the Iranian Revolution.[7] Immediately after the new regime assumed control of the country in 1979, Ayatollah Khomeini—the leader of the revolution and the founder of the Islamic Republic of Iran—banned music from the Iranian radio and television (Kifner,

---

[6] Naser Khosrow (1004–1088) was a Persian poet and philosopher. This ode reminds me of the idiom "You have made your bed and now you have to lie in it."

[7] "Revolution," in *The Merriam-Webster Dictionary*, https://www.merriam-webster.com/dictionary/revolution

1979; Seyedsayamdost, 2017).[8] His *fatwā* against *motreb's* music was in harmony with other *fuqahā*. They all agreed that *Motrebi* music is sinful and forbidden by the Islamic law (*harām*).[9] In his meeting with the staff of *Radio Darya*—a popular radio station before the revolution—in 1979, Ayatollah Khomeini declared, "... youths who spend their time listening to music can no longer appreciate realities, just as a drug addict cannot.... Music is a betrayal of the nation and of youth.... Eliminate it altogether" (Hamedani, 2017, 21:53; Youssefzadeh, 2000, p. 38). On February 12, 1979, the Islamic Revolutionary Council appointed Sadegh Ghotbzadeh, a prominent Iranian political figure and revolutionary, as the head of the National Iranian Radio and Television (NIRT, which became IRIB after the revolution).[10] On July 24, 1979, under

---

[8] Ayatollah Khomeini (1902–1989) also known as Imam Khomeini (or simply Imam) inside Iran and by his supporters internationally, was a leader of the 1979 Revolution.

[9] *Fatwā* is an Islamic legal ruling given by qualified Islamic Jurists in response to questions from private individuals, judges or governments. A *Faqīh* (plural: *fuqahā*) is an expert in Islamic law. In Islam, when an authorized top-ranking clergy issues a fatwā, it is obligatory for all Muslims who follow that clergy to adhere to it. In the absence of *fatwā* on a specific matter, *ijmā'* (consensus among scholars) is to be followed, particularly the ruling of most top-ranking clerics. However, some matters do not need *fatwā* or *ijmā'*. In such cases, societal morals are to be referenced, which may vary over time across different societies. "*Motreb* is applied only to musicians who perform at weddings, parties, and other festive events. The term *motreb* is closely linked to a form of performance known as *ruhowsi*, which also emerged at the beginning of the twentieth century ... which did not survive the 1979 revolution." (Breyley and Fatemi, 2016)

[10] National Iranian Radio and Television (*radio o televizion-e melli-e Iran*, NIRT) was the first Iranian state broadcaster, which was established on June 19, 1971, operated up until the Iranian Revolution in 1979—after the revolution it became the Islamic Republic of Iran Broadcasting (IRIB). Islamic Republic of Iran Broadcasting (*Sedā o Simā*, IRIB) is an Iranian media corporation that holds a monopoly of domestic radio and television services in Iran after the

the supreme leader's direction he issued a decree banning music from the country's radio and television stations during Ramadan, except revolutionary songs and marches.[11] Accordingly, Abdolrahim Mokri—the supervisor of the music department of IRIB (*Sedā o Simā*)—ordered producers to limit music broadcast until further notice. He also provided a list of approved revolutionary marches ("*Ruzi ke paxš-e musiqi az radio o televizion qad-e qan shod*," 2019).

Revolutionary songs gained popularity among political and opposition groups protesting against the *Shāh* of Iran.[12] Many of those melodies were adapted from social movements and partisan songs originating from Latin American countries. For instance, "*Barpāxiz*" [Arise] was inspired by the internationally renowned song of the 'New Chilean Song' movement, 'El pueblo unido jamás será vencido' (Hosseini, 2016, 10:00).[13] Demonstrators fervently sang these revolutionary anthems, symbolizing the nation's resistance against aristocracy and suppression both before and after the revolution. A notable example occurred during Ayatollah Khomeini's welcome ceremony upon his return to Iran after fourteen years in exile on February 1st, 1979. Songwriter

---

revolution. It is independent of the Iranian government, but its head is directly appointed by the supreme leader of Iran.
[11] Ramadan is the ninth month of the lunar calendar, observed by Muslims worldwide as a month of fasting and prayer.
[12] Mohammad Reza Pahlavi (1919 –1980), a.k.a Mohammad Reza Shah, was the last *Shāh* (Emperor) of Iran from 1941 until his overthrow in the Iranian Revolution in 1979.
[13] Kankash. (2018, January 20). *Sorud-e Barpāxiz* [Video file]. Retrieved from https://youtu.be/JYDNITSy5-Y

Hamid Shahangian formed a men's chorus, known as *goruh-e sorud* [vocal ensemble], comprising volunteers, including non-professional vocalists, to perform Shahangian's revolutionary song: '*Khomeini Ey Imam*' ['Khomeini, O Imam'] at Mehrabad Airport, where Ayatollah Khomeini's plane landed. (ibid., 9:26)[14]

However, some revolutionaries considered all kinds of music forbidden. As Bijan Kamkar recalls, "Beside setting fire to liquor stores and movie theaters, they [revolutionaries] burnt stores which sold music cassettes and recordings; one may find it hard to believe if he had not witnessed those events" (Hosseini, 2016, 18:05).[15] Kambiz Roshanravan mentions, "Music [in Iran] was suspended in 1979–1980" (ibid., 22:10).[16] Hamid Shahangian—the head of the IRIB Sorud Centre (*Markaz-e Sorud-e Sedā o Simā*) between 1980–83—adds, "At the time, *Hawza* put a strong pressure on us to stop broadcasting music since it is *harām* [forbidden by Islamic law]" (ibid., 22:46).[17] Yet, Mehdi Kalhor—the head of IRIB Sorud Centre between 1984–87—believed the real reason behind the *fatwā*

---

[14] '*Khomeini Ey Imam*' is a famous Iranian revolutionary song praising Ayatollah Khomeini. The historical performance at Mehrabad Airport, where Imam Khomeini's plane landed, can be viewed at: Eastern Earth. (2021, September 2) *Khomeini Ey Imam Sorud* [Video File]. Retrieved from https://www.youtube.com/watch?v=xrYR9_c_6g8

[15] Bijan Kamkar (born 1949) is an Iranian Kurdish musician. He is a Persian traditional music (*musiqi-e asil-e Irani*) singer, and also *tār*, *tombak* and *daf* player.
See https://khabarfarsi.com/u/61771948

[16] Kambiz Roshanravan (born 1949) is an Iranian composer, music educator, and flutist.

[17] *Hawza* is a seminary where Shi'a Muslim clerics are educated.

was not necessarily the Islamic law. He says, "The attitude against music was rooted in and reflected [some] religious people's bias against music. They disapproved of and avoided NIRT programs before the revolution" (ibid., 22:57). He continues, "Imam [Ayatollah Khoemini] mentioned that during his visit to Qom in 1979, a Muslim cleric asked him to ban music broadcast on [IRIB] Radio since it was *harām*. "I answered", Imam said, "You cannot control radio broadcast programs, but you can control radio [receiver] knobs [Just turn it off]" (ibid., 25:45). Kalhor then adds, "Some did not even listen to the News intro music—a short Islamic march.[18] They turned off the television and turned it back on after the tune was over. We followed Imam's guidance, and other people's thinking did not affect our decision" (ibid., 26:01).

The 1980s marked a perilous time for music and musicians in Iran. The establishment of the government-backed ideological organization, *Dāyere-ye Mobāreze bā Monkarāt* [Department of Combatting Vice], heightened the scrutiny of activities deemed contrary to Islamic law. Among its objectives was the confiscation of music cassettes and recordings labeled as vulgar music, *musiqi-e mobtazal*, a categorization that could be applied to various music genres. Additionally, musical instruments, referred to as *ālāt o adavāt-e musiqi*, were targeted

---

[18] "*Mā Mosallah be Allāh-o Akbarim*" [we are armed with Allahu Akbar] was an Islamic marching song. For more than three decades, it has been the intro music for Iranian television news across all channels and hours. You can watch a performance of this marching song in the presence of Imam Khomeini at https://www.aparat.com/v/s42b3s7

for confiscation.[19] Confiscated music cassettes underwent destruction or erasure. After removing vulgar music, *musiqi-e mobtazal,* from the tapes, the blank audio cassettes were presented to mosques and Islamic Development Organization, *Sāzmān-e Tabliqāt-e Islāmi,* to be reused for religious purposes, such as recordings of the Quranic recitations or prayers. Similarly, confiscated musical instruments were either destroyed outright or repurposed for religious or military use by the Islamic Republic of Iran's Army or *Sepāh.*[20] Despite the risks involved, some individuals engaged in illicit activities, such as copying and selling illegal music. For instance, the ninth album of Kiosk, an Iranian rock band formed in Tehran in 2003, narrates the story of Kamran Mellat, who established an underground network called Stereo Tull to duplicate and distribute Western pop music (Razi, 2016).[21] After nearly a decade of his operating underground, authorities apprehended Mellat's sister, compelling him to surrender (Keshtkar, 2016).

Moreover, Imam Khomeini promptly ordered the establishment of a militia, known as the Islamic Revolution Committees, or simply *Komite,* one day after the revolution. Tasked with enforcing Islamic law and morality in society,

---

[19] After the revolution, Arabic terminology like 'ālāt o adavāt' began to be favored in official discourse over the traditional Persian term '*sāz*' indicating a shift in terminology in official contexts.
[20] The Army of Guardians of the Islamic Revolution (*Sepāh*) is a branch of the Iranian Armed Forces, operating independently from the regular armed forces. It was founded after the Iranian Revolution by the order of Ayatollah Khomeini.
[21] The name of the band, *Kiosk,* stems from the original formation of the group in Tehran, when its members gathered together in any possible makeshift space or "kiosk" to play their music without fear of arrest.

these committees wielded significant power. Hossein Alizadeh, a former revolutionary and dedicated composer, recounts his experience:

> Members of the Komite, our fellow citizens and acquaintances, were armed and empowered to enforce their directives against us. They would intercept our vehicles at night, brandishing weapons and demanding we open the trunk. Encountering musical instruments, they treated us as though we were dangerous criminals. (Hosseini, 2016, 50:28)[22]

Consequently, professional musicians were required to obtain written permits, known as *mojavvez*, from authorities to transport their musical instruments, akin to firearms licenses (see Appendix A). These permits granted musicians the right to possess and carry their musical instruments, cassette tapes, and music recorders for the performance and recording of revolutionary songs.

Homayoun Rahimian, a composer, reflects on the early post-revolutionary years: "I witnessed a *Komite* member once intercepting an individual carrying a musical instrument, only to kick and damage it upon discovery" (Hosseini, 2016, 49:42).[23] Rahimian further recalls expressing frustration to authorities about the futility of the permit: "I argued that the

---

[22] Hossein Alizadeh (born 1951) is an Iranian composer and *tār* player.
[23] Homayoun Rahimian (born 1954) is an Iranian composer and violin player.

permit to carry musical instruments was meaningless, as my instrument would often be damaged before I could even present it for inspection (ibid., 51:12). He recounts another troubling incident from that era:

> *Komite* members at the entrance of the IRIB's *Herāsat* stopped me and inquired about my musical instrument sarcastically, 'I see that you are once again bringing your musical instruments (*mizqun pizqun*[24])?' I replied, 'These revolutionary songs and marches which you hear [on IRIB] are played with THESE MUSICAL INSTRUMENTS not with pots and saucepans (*bā qāblāme ke nemizanan, BĀ INE*).'[25] (ibid., 49:58)

Some musicians emerged as fervent revolutionaries during this period. Prior to the revolution, a group of traditional musicians adjusted the festive (*bazmi*) spirit and structure of Persian traditional music (*musiqi-e asil-e Irani*) to epic and revolutionary (*razmi*). Bijan Kamkar explains, "Persian [traditional] music was inherently celebratory, *bazmi*, not suitable for large-scale performances at concert halls, but best suited for intimate gatherings due to the limitations of Persian musical instruments" (Hosseini, 2016, 11:03). *Sheida and Aref*

---

[24] A vulgar expression for humiliating musical instruments.
[25] The Iranian government established *Herāsat* (security offices) at all public organizations after the revolution. *Herāsat* functions under the direct supervision of the Ministry of Intelligence. Some of their main assignments are to monitor, stop, and report to the authorities any activities that violate Islamic law.

these committees wielded significant power. Hossein Alizadeh, a former revolutionary and dedicated composer, recounts his experience:

> Members of the Komite, our fellow citizens and acquaintances, were armed and empowered to enforce their directives against us. They would intercept our vehicles at night, brandishing weapons and demanding we open the trunk. Encountering musical instruments, they treated us as though we were dangerous criminals. (Hosseini, 2016, 50:28)[22]

Consequently, professional musicians were required to obtain written permits, known as *mojavvez*, from authorities to transport their musical instruments, akin to firearms licenses (see Appendix A). These permits granted musicians the right to possess and carry their musical instruments, cassette tapes, and music recorders for the performance and recording of revolutionary songs.

Homayoun Rahimian, a composer, reflects on the early post-revolutionary years: "I witnessed a *Komite* member once intercepting an individual carrying a musical instrument, only to kick and damage it upon discovery" (Hosseini, 2016, 49:42).[23] Rahimian further recalls expressing frustration to authorities about the futility of the permit: "I argued that the

---

[22] Hossein Alizadeh (born 1951) is an Iranian composer and *tār* player.
[23] Homayoun Rahimian (born 1954) is an Iranian composer and violin player.

permit to carry musical instruments was meaningless, as my instrument would often be damaged before I could even present it for inspection (ibid., 51:12). He recounts another troubling incident from that era:

> *Komite* members at the entrance of the IRIB's *Herāsat* stopped me and inquired about my musical instrument sarcastically, 'I see that you are once again bringing your musical instruments (*mizqun pizqun*[24])?' I replied, 'These revolutionary songs and marches which you hear [on IRIB] are played with THESE MUSICAL INSTRUMENTS not with pots and saucepans (*bā qāblāme ke nemizanan, BĀ INE*).'[25] (ibid., 49:58)

Some musicians emerged as fervent revolutionaries during this period. Prior to the revolution, a group of traditional musicians adjusted the festive (*bazmi*) spirit and structure of Persian traditional music (*musiqi-e asil-e Irani*) to epic and revolutionary (*razmi*). Bijan Kamkar explains, "Persian [traditional] music was inherently celebratory, *bazmi*, not suitable for large-scale performances at concert halls, but best suited for intimate gatherings due to the limitations of Persian musical instruments" (Hosseini, 2016, 11:03). *Sheida and Aref*

---

[24] A vulgar expression for humiliating musical instruments.
[25] The Iranian government established *Herāsat* (security offices) at all public organizations after the revolution. *Herāsat* functions under the direct supervision of the Ministry of Intelligence. Some of their main assignments are to monitor, stop, and report to the authorities any activities that violate Islamic law.

Ensembles (later renamed to *Chavosh* after 1978) introduced choral elements to their ensemble for the first time, amplifying their revolutionary sentiments and epic narratives. However, they did not sustain this unconventional approach to manipulating Persian traditional music (*musiqi-e asil-e Irani*) in subsequent years.

Hossein Alizadeh reminisces, "[During the revolution,] we composed, performed and recorded our music hastily. Our recordings were made at home; at times, you could hear the faint cries of infants in the background" (ibid., 17:30). Subsequently, the Kamkars (primarily their father) reproduced copies of these original recordings using audio cassette tape duplicators.[26] Alizadeh elaborates:

> The next day, we divided into small groups and sold these cassettes directly to people, often in specific districts of Tehran. To attract buyers, we occasionally played the recordings aloud in our cars or on boomboxes in the streets. During those tumultuous times, society was in upheaval, and we were passionate about creating revolutionary songs [quickly]. Though simple and even amateurish upon listening, they were sincere expressions of our convictions (ibid., 18:40).

---

[26] The Kamkars are a Kurdish family and ensemble consisting of seven brothers and one sister. The group has performed numerous concerts around the world.

This group of musicians represented a substantial portion of Iranian society at the time, sharing a collective belief in the ideals of the revolution. They envisioned a democratic government system and embraced the promise of a liberal utopia championed by the revolution. Consequently, they rallied behind Ayatollah Khomeini, viewing him as a spiritual leader capable of toppling the Shāh. However, disillusionment soon pervaded their ranks. Shahangian notes, "We witnessed the exodus of nearly all musicians. Those who remained did so out of personal conviction and various other considerations" (Hosseini, 2016, 1:55:45). As a result, a significant number of musicians chose to leave Iran during or after the revolution. Alizadeh reflects, "I felt a sense of futility in persevering amidst the numerous obstacles facing [Iran's] music.... Hence, I made the decision to temporarily leave the country" (ibid., 1:55:11).

After the revolution, professional musicians found themselves unemployed, losing their positions at various cultural organizations like the Iranian National Ballet and Opera Company. Some opted to become full-time stay-at-home musicians, while others made the difficult decision to leave their homeland. Even those initially hailed as revolutionaries soon found themselves labeled as "*chappī*" (leftist) or "*toudeh-ī*" (members of an Iranian communist party), leading to their exclusion, dismissal, and being barred from employment for several years, particularly at public and government institutions. Composers faced particularly dire circumstances, with limited opportunities available to them. Many felt compelled to cooperate with IRIB (*Sedā o Simā*) and *Ershād*,[27] although they were reluctant to do so. As Shahangian remarked during an interview in 2017:

> Although numerous skilled musicians remained in the country in 1979, there was a scarcity of composers willing to create revolutionary songs for IRIB (*Sedā o Simā*). This reluctance stemmed from the fact that many musicians did not inherently believe in the revolution or share its values (Rahimi, 2017a, para. 7).

Before the 1979 Revolution, particularly from the 1950s to the late 1970s, music flourished across Iran, with vibrant performances and educational programs in concert halls, schools, and universities. Additionally, radio, television, entertainment centers, bars, and nightclubs in major cities hosted a diverse array of music and performing arts programs. However, the landscape drastically changed immediately after the revolution. Live music and concerts came to an abrupt halt, exemplified by the closure of Roudaki Hall, *Talar-e Roudaki*, a prominent performing arts complex in Tehran established in 1967. Following the revolution, the hall ceased all music programs, including opera and ballet productions. Moreover, revolutionaries invaded the hall, where they proceeded to stack and burn costumes, books, and scores in the front yard

---

[27] The Ministry of Culture and Islamic Guidance (*Vezārat-e Farhang o Ershād-e Eslāmi*) is simply known as *Ershād*.

(Hamedani, 2017, 22:40). Mahmoud Khoshnam describes a meeting between top clerics of Qom's *Hawza* and cultural council officials to scrutinize the previous cultural guidelines, and determine and establish new policies.[28] Khoshnam states:

> After participants discussed the agenda in minute detail, I raised my hand to request permission to speak as the representative of the Roudaki Hall. After permission was granted, I asked, what will happen to the ballet and opera of the country? My question made the clergy fly into a rage. Infuriated and fuming he retorted, are you not embarrassed? Islamic Republic [of Iran] and ballet. It is ridiculous. (ibid., 22:51)

The invasion of the Rudaki Hall was not the only aggression towards music and music organizations during those days. As Shahangian recounts:

> Bastard *Monafeghin* took this opportunity to storm the IRIB (*Sedā o Simā*) and piled the archive recordings of NIRT Radio in the yard to burn them.[29] I was shouting, running and begging them to stop [destroying our history].... I cried out, these will be supporting evidence

---

[28] Mahmoud Khoshnam (1935-2021) was a Persian music critic and the deputy artistic director of *Rudaki Hall* before the revolution.
[29] "Mojahedin-e Khalq," also denounced as "Monafeghin" according to Islamic Republic officials, is an Iranian political-militant organization. This group initially supported the revolution but later became an opposition group against the Islamic Republic system.

if after thirty years we need proof of how vulgar music has been before the revolution. Let's preserve the archive to prove to the next generation that our [IRIB's] productions are superior to theirs [*Pahlavi*s]. Alas, in hindsight it turned out the other way around—theirs proved to be superior. (Hosseini, 2016, 23:16)

It is worthwhile to cite two other accounts of similar incidents, one from my first piano teacher and another from a violin maestro.

In the late 1980s, my first piano teacher, who also worked in the NIRT Radio archive department, told us he sensed the ominous situation during the early days after the revolution. As a precautionary action, he moved archival materials to a secure place and built a false wall to hide them. He managed to do this despite the fact that he suffered from a severe mobility disorder.

The second account, by a violinist whom my parents met at a private gathering, may present another version of Shahangian's story. In this version of the story, a notorious radical Muslim cleric accompanied by a crowd of revolutionaries came to burn all the music recordings at the IRIB building. As a last resort, one of the Radio employees begged them to listen to one of their recent recordings called "*Shahid-e Motahar*" [purified martyr] before destroying the entire archive.[30] The employee promised to pile and burn all the

---

[30] Martyr Ayatollah Morteza Motahari. (2016, July 1). *Shahid-e Motahar* [Video file]. Retrieved from https://youtu.be/qjbuGZgIqWM

archival materials himself, if they deemed the recording to go against their beliefs. The authorities had commissioned "*Shahid-e Motahar*" for the first anniversary of the martyrdom of Morteza Motahari, but IRIB did not broadcast it.[31] The clergy was so impressed that he listened to the recording three times. He then ordered the archive to be preserved and left the building (see Appendix B and Appendix C).

A few weeks later, on June 15, 1980, in a meeting with the senior managers of IRIB Radio, Ayatollah Khomeini made a statement for the first time that utterly negated his previous rebuke of music. He stated:

> As I have pointed out since the very early days of the uprising, if you want to reform the society you have to reform [NIRT] radio and television. One of the radio directors mentioned, 'Actually there have been no *sorud* (anthem or hymn) productions about God, Allah, Imam, and the [Iran's] Islamic Revolution. So we are fulfilling our duty here by producing these kinds of *soruds*.' Ayatollah Khomeini replied, 'These kinds of sensational and beneficial *soruds* cause no problem.' Someone interrupted him, 'Like the *sorud* of Mr. Motahari?' The Imam added, '*Sorud* of Mr. Motahari causes no problem.' (Hosseini, 2016, 24:32).

---

[31] Morteza Motahari was a prominent Iranian cleric who was assassinated on May 1, 1979.

Ayatollah Khomeini's confirmation had a great impact on musicians at IRIB. Shahangian points out, "Imam's approval of *'Shahid-e Motahar' sorud* paved the way for his team in radio to move ahead [and produce more *soruds* at IRIB (*Sedā o Simā*)]" (Hosseini, 2016, 25:05). Shahangian adds, "The ensemble consisted of different musical instruments such as *tār*, *tanbur*, and violin—all were forbidden.[32] Then, why is the combination not *harām*? Lyrics overshadow music" (ibid., 25:26). Interestingly, this *sorud* was originally composed for Hayedeh, one of the most popular female vocalists of Iran, whose music was forbidden after the revolution. In *"Shahid-e Motahar"*, the composer had even recorded all instrumental parts, but Hayedeh was not available to record the vocals—perhaps due to the fact that she had left Iran in August 1978 during the turmoil. Consequently, when the composer received the commission a few years later in 1980, he added new lyrics and asked a male singer to perform, since female solo performance was no longer permitted under Islamic law. Mohammad Golriz, the singer of *"Shahid-e Motahar"* adds, "Imam [Khomeini] said, I listen to this *sorud* here [on IRIB radio], but I would not listen, were it played on *Voice of America*" ("Some singers do not," 2013).

---

[32] *Tār* is an Iranian long-necked, plucked string instrument, shared by many cultures and countries including Iran, Azerbaijan, Armenia, Georgia, and others near the Caucasus region.

The Rise of Artwashing, Censorship, Exploitation, and Demagoguery

ما شاهد سقوط حقیقت،
ما شاهد تلاشی انسان،
ما صاحبان واقعه بودیم،
چندی به زجر، شعله کشیدیم،
وینک درون خاطره دودیم.
گفتند:"رو به اوج روانیم."
دیدیم سیر سوی هبوط است،
شعر سپید نیست، که خوانیش،
این جعبه‌ی سیاه سقوط است.

محمدرضا شفیعی کدکنی

Witnesses to the truth's descent,
Witnesses to the humanity's downfall,
We bore the event's burden,
For a time, in agony's blaze, we suffered,
Now, within memory, we turn to smoke.
They said: "we ascend towards the peak."
We saw the trend is towards descent.
This isn't a white poetry to be recited,[33]
This is the black box of the crash.

Mohammad-Reza Shafiei-Kadkani[34]

---

[33] *Sepid* poetry (sepid, "white") refers to a free verse movement in Modern Persian poetry characterized by its departure from Classical Persian prosody and its embrace of new content, viewpoint, and diction.

[34] Dr. Mohammad-Reza Shafiei-Kadkani (born 1939) is an Iranian poet, author, literary critic, and professor of literature at Tehran University.

The authorities' contradictory statements about music, coupled with their substitution of the term "music" (*musiqi*) with the unconventional term "*sorud*," illustrate the exploitation of music for self-serving purposes. In essence, they used "beneficial *sorud*" as a metaphor for music productions that supported and promoted the regime's propaganda.

Music was declared *harām* [forbidden by Islamic law] unless approved by authorities appointed by the regime. Consequently, familiar terms used to describe music, such as "*musiqi*" [music], "*taraneh*" [song], and "*tasnif*" [chanson], were replaced with the term "*sorud*" [anthem or hymn]—perhaps to associate music solely with religion and revolution. Roshanravan highlights that, "Over ninety-five percent of all IRIB (*Sedā o Simā*) [music] productions cannot be referred to as *sorud*" (Hosseini, 2016, 29:09). However, the falsification was apparently effective. Alizadeh points out:

> In my view, it was demagoguery. Instead of informing and educating the general public through rational arguments, authorities sometimes resort to seeking support by stooping to the level of uninformed individuals. If the term "music" unsettles them, the authorities simply label it as "*sorud*." By doing so, the product ceases to be perceived as music (deemed *harām* in their minds) and instead appears legitimate as "*sorud*" (ibid., 29:38).

The authorities not only substituted the term "music" to "*sorud*", but also prefixed "revolutionary songs" to "*sorud*". According to Majid Derakhshani, "This addition of 'revolutionary' bestowed a sense of sanctity upon the music. Additionally, the government altered the name of the 'Ershād Music Centre' to 'Ershād Sorud and Revolutionary Songs Centre'" (Hosseini, 2016, 30:14).[35] Subsequently, in 1984, Ershād went further by renaming the Tehran Conservatory of Music as part of efforts to obtain permission from the authorities for its reopening. They divided the conservatory into two separate schools, one for boys and one for girls, each located in different areas of Tehran: Sorud and Revolutionary Songs Conservatory–Boys Centre, and Sorud and Revolutionary Songs Conservatory–Girls Centre (see Appendix D).

The IRIB Sorud Centre and Ershād Sorud Centre manipulated terms and language to serve their own interests. However, their exploitation did not end there. IRIB (*Sedā o Simā*) utilized musicians' compositions on television and radio without compensating them. Despite receiving a substantial budget from the government and generating significant revenue from advertisements commissioned by the private sector, IRIB does not pay any royalties to independent musicians whose works are aired on its media platforms. Some notable artists, such as Shajarian and Farhad, have filed lawsuits against

---

[35] Majid Derakhshani (born 1957) is an Iranian composer and *tār* player.

IRIB.³⁶ Nevertheless, IRIB managers countered these claims by arguing that musicians benefit from the exposure and recognition gained when their music is broadcast on national media ("Javāb-e moštarak-e Sedā o Simā," 2018).

Alizadeh's composition *Neynava*, written for *ney* and string orchestra, stood out as an exception.³⁷ Following its release in 1983, IRIB paid Alizadeh for the broadcasting rights of his work on IRIB Radio. The audience's response to this piece was unprecedentedly positive. In fact, it marked the first time after the revolution that people queued up to purchase a music record. Alizadeh recalls the aftermath:

> After the immense success of *Neynava*, a director of IRIB Radio summoned me to his office and urged me to compose a piece of music glorifying the [military operation of] *Fath-ol-Mobin*. He assured me they were prepared to pay any price for such a composition. At that time, I was only thirty-two years old, seated in front of an old *Hāj-Āqā*.³⁸ I replied that our perceptions of war differed. I couldn't articulate my emotions; I simply stated, 'I perceive the horrors of war. [For instance,] what follows after a bomb drops? [Destruction and

---

³⁶ Mohammad-Reza Shajarian (1940–2020) was a renowned Iranian singer and master of Persian traditional music (*musiqi-e asil-e Irani*). Farhad Mehrad (1944–2002) was a renowned Iranian pop singer.
³⁷ *Ney* is an ancient Persian end-blown flute.
³⁸ A man (*āqā*) who has done Hajj, Muslims' pilgrimage to Mecca, is sometimes called "*Hāj-Āqā*." Sometimes people may address a male stranger as "*Hāj-Āqā*" instead of just "*Āqā*" as a show of respect among Muslims, but in certain contexts it can imply a position of authority.

devastation.] That's my understanding of war.' He retorted, 'And?' I replied, 'Well, that's the essence of *Neynava*' (Hosseini, 2016, 1:43:07).

During the Iran-Iraq war, IRIB (*Sedā o Simā*) and Ershād enlisted a team of musicians to compose and perform *soruds*. The IRIB Sorud Centre worked closely with artists to produce a substantial collection of epic musical compositions glorifying the war. These epic songs served as a form of pro-war propaganda, encouraging citizens to volunteer for the armed forces. Hamidreza Khazaei, the manager of *Radio Jebheh* [Battlefield Radio Station] during the war, states:[39]

> We had to prioritize the best interests of the Islamic Republic of Iran and adjust verses and lines accordingly, even if it meant compromising the original work to some extent..... The IRIB Sorud Centre council stressed that the focus should not solely be on Iran and the homeland. For instance, they criticized a work for placing too much emphasis on nationality and patriotism, suggesting instead that we highlight the Islamic Republic without exceeding this focus (Hosseini, 2016, 1:56:54, 2:00:24).

---

[39] *Radio Jebheh* was a public radio station that was established in 1985 to broadcast the latest news and information about the Iran-Iraq war. It operated up until the end of the war in 1988.

Despite efforts to navigate the restrictions, musicians and music productions continued to face significant pressure from *Hawza*, hard-liners, and the pro-regime forces, who viewed music as a symbol of aristocracy or deviance. Bijan Kamkar recalls:

> In one instance, we received all required permissions from top-ranking government authorities to [publicly] perform music at the University of Tehran. Just one *basiji* at *Honarhā-ye Zibā* (the art department at the University of Tehran) disagreed and stopped our performance.[40] He argued that we were *'Chappi'*. We objected to this unsubstantiated comment and indicated that we honestly intended to perform music. He retorted that he did not want *Chappis'* honesty (Hosseini, 2016, 38:26).

After the revolution, artists continued to grapple with censorship under the new regime's stringent regulations. Notably, Nosrat Karimi faced prohibitions on his work as a filmmaker, actor, and even as a teacher at film schools.[41] He was arrested and sentenced to death for his romantic comedy movie 'The Interim Husband,' screened in 1971, years before the revolution.[42] Following a brief period of imprisonment, he

---

[40] *Basij* is a paramilitary civilian volunteer-based youth militia organization established in Iran by the order of Ayatollah Khomeini in 1979. Members of *Basij* are called *Basiji*.
[41] Nosrat Karimi (1924-2019) was a renowned and progressive filmmaker, who challenged dogmatic religious rules about marriage and social life in his films.
[42] BBC Persian. (2019, December 10). *Aparat–Bozorgdāšt-e Nosrat Karimi dar mostanade Zendegi* [Aparat–Commemoration of Nosrat Karimi in 'Life' documentary; Video file]. https://youtu.be/rlPVVUioZk4

was pardoned by Imam Khomeini. However, Ayatollah Gilani, the chief judge of Tehran's Islamic revolutionary court from 1980 to 1985, compelled him to write an open letter of repentance for publication in newspapers.

After his release, Karimi sustained himself by cultivating cactus plants and expressing his artistic vision through sculpting busts at home.[43] These portrait sculptures symbolize the impact of censorship, reflecting the roles he desired to play and the films he wished to direct. It is as if each of these hundred little faces, with a silent language, narrates the stories of Nosrat's characters. They, silent witnesses to his artistic struggle, serve as a poignant reminder of the enduring impact of censorship on Iranian artists.

His apprehension is evident in an interview for the documentary '*Zendegi*' (life) (Mohseni, 2005), where he requests the director to omit any mention of his brush with death, fearing it could reignite authorities' interest in his case. Karimi, like many eminent artists, found solace in self-imposed exile at home. While he adapted to solitude, many others succumbed to depression.

Occasionally, prominent clergies and authorities issued ambiguous statements to relax the restrictions on music. For instance, on January 10, 1986, Hujjat-al-Islam Ali Khamenei,

---

[43] A bust is a sculptural representation of a person's head, neck, and sometimes shoulders and chest, typically created from materials like marble, bronze, or clay, and intended for display as an artwork or monument.

who was the president of Iran at the time, formally declared during his Friday Prayer sermon, *khotbeh*, in Tehran:

> Some might wonder why art is being discussed in this sacred setting of Friday prayer. Let me briefly clarify that art, by its nature, is sacred, and the presentation of *āhanghā-ye xošk* ['dry songs' or perhaps 'Songs that are not entertaining'] that adheres to Sharia principles is a form of art—a commendable one.[44] Not all pre-revolution artists are malevolent; a good song that complies with Islamic law can be more impactful than dozens of speeches[45] (ibid., 52:59).

This selective endorsement of art and music can be seen as part of broader efforts by the regime to control and shape cultural production. Such efforts are sometimes referred to artwashing. Artwashing involves the practice of promoting state-approved art in order to improve public perception, while also serving to obscure controversial or oppressive actions. In the context of post-revolution Iran, this meant highlighting certain artistic expressions while censoring others, thereby managing the cultural narrative.

---

[44] Sharia: Islamic law derived from the Quran and Hadith.
[45] Tehran's Friday Prayer is the most important public congregational prayer held by the regime every Friday. Prior to praying, an influential authority explains the regime's opinion about different issues, an address called a sermon (*Khotbeh*).

Some musicians still struggle to grasp the precise criteria used to classify music and musicians as either good or evil. Khoshnam shares his perplexity, stating:

> The approach of mullahs' [Muslim clerics] to music is perplexing to me. Regardless of whether their viewpoint is correct or not, their stance on music remains entirely incomprehensible. For instance, they argue that music is acceptable if used for mourning, but otherwise, it is deemed offensive (*makruh*) (Hamedani, 2017, 22:12).

The government's stance, policies, and directives concerning music exhibit significant contradictions. Arsalan Kamkar, the concertmaster at Tehran Symphony Orchestra (TSO), highlights this inconsistency, stating:

> After 1979, the TSO's repertoire was restricted to revolutionary songs for a duration of six years. Even classical music was prohibited for the initial five to six years. During this period, not only were we deprived of any budgetary allocation, but the very existence of the TSO was precarious and uncertain. In order to demonstrate our alignment with the [1979] revolution and to ensure our survival, we exclusively performed revolutionary songs at official events (Rahimi, 2017b, para. 15).

Despite the TSO's unwavering commitment, the government failed to accord it due respect. Throughout this period, authorities frequently deployed TSO members to perform in war zones without providing any compensation upon completion of their duties (see Appendix E). Arsalan Kamkar further elaborates, stating, "Every year, we were requested to perform on the anniversary of the [1979] Revolution. However, following the ceremony, the authorities often neglected to arrange for the TSO's payment. Moreover, they consistently failed to allocate a budget to support the TSO" (Rahimi, 2017b, para.17) (see Appendix F).

The contradictory stance towards music persisted prominently in the initial years post-revolution. While challenges persist for Iranian musicians and performers today, the stringent restrictions endured during the early years were particularly severe. Roshanravan highlights this paradox, stating, "Signing contracts with composers was deemed a sin under Islamic law (*man'e shar'i va ma'siyat dār-e*.) Yet, IRIB (*Sedā o Simā*) utilized their music in various programs" (Hosseini, 2016, 49:14; Youssefzadeh, 2000, p. 38). As a result, composers not only had to halt their professional pursuits but were also hesitant to even mention the word "music." Hooshang Javid reflects on this, likening the use of the term "music" to carrying out a suicidal attack with dynamite, as perceived by pro-regime extremists" (Hosseini, 2016, 49:27).[46]

---

[46] Hooshang Javid (born 1959) is an Iranian ethnomusicologist.

The authorities, facing uncertainty, looked to Ayatollah Khomeini for clarity on music regulations, but he chose not to offer a definitive answer. For instance, in 1987, Nader Kojuri, director of *Ershād-e Fars*, requested a *fatwā* from Ayatollah Khomeini due to the ambiguity of his previous ruling on music.[47] Kojuri's two-page official letter began with customary invocation of God's name and characterized by an exceedingly respectful tone towards Ayatollah Khomeini, the Supreme Leader. In his letter, Kojuri expressed apologies for troubling Ayatollah Khomeini with what he perceived as a trivial matter—music. He concluded by posing a direct query, recalling Khomeini's previous declaration regarding the classification of motreb's music as *harām* [forbidden by Islamic law], contrasted with sounds of questionable origins (*sedāhāy-e maśkuk*). Kojuri sought clarification on who had the authority to determine such criteria. In response to Kojuri's extensive letter, Ayatollah Khomeini's reply was surprisingly succinct: "In the name of God, it is mores (*orfi ast*) [social norms determine it]". With just two words, he delegated the determination of music's permissibility to "social norms" (Kojuri, 2018, paras. 4–5).

Ayatollah Khomeini declined to issue a direct instruction or *fatwā* to differentiate between *harām* and *halāl* music, citing the abstract nature of music itself.[48] The precise boundary

---

[47] Ershād-e Fārs: Refers to the provincial branch of the Ershād organization in Iran, located in the Fārs province.
[48] *Halāl* means permissible by Islamic law.

between permissible and forbidden music remains elusive, as it hinges on various factors such as the composer's intent, the lyrical content, and the audience's response. This ambiguity creates opportunities for exploitation, allowing opportunistic individuals to exploit music that straddles the borderland between *harām* and *halāl*. For instance, during the 1980s, a council of poets and musicians convened at the IRIB Sorud Centre, selectively commissioning a limited number of composers to create war marches. These works required the council's approval at every stage, from the initial creation to the final product, ensuring strict adherence to the regime's guidelines for every single word and note.

The ban on displaying musical instruments on IRIB (*Sedā o Simā*) has persisted for over four decades, with few exceptions. In 1987, two unprecedented music performances broke this norm. Firstly, the *Abadeh Boys Chorus* was invited to perform at *Jamaran Hussainia* before Ayatollah Khomeini, clerics, and religious extremists.[49] The presence of an electronic organ and *ney* alongside the choir in the holy presence of Imam Khomeini and his associates made this event unimaginable.[50] Even more intriguing, Ahmad Khomeini, Ayatollah Khomeini's son and close confidant, instructed IRIB to not only record the event but also focus cameras on the musical

---

[49] *Jamaran Hussainia* was a congregational hall linked to Ayatollah Khomeini's residency. Ayatollah Khomeini often walked up a flight of stairs leading from his house to the balcony of the *hussainia*, from which he often spoke.

[50] You can watch the performance of The *Abadeh Boys Chorus* at Jamaran Hussainia before Ayatollah Khomeini, clerics, and religious extremists at https://www.aparat.com/v/H0uKY

instruments and choir, broadcasting the performance nationwide on the same night. Mehdi Nazari, the vocal soloist at *Abadeh Boys Chorus* and a young boy at the time, vividly recalls the event:

> I had a lump in my throat. I cannot explain why. It was a heavy atmosphere. Imam [Khomeini] was sitting on the balcony. I, a child, dared to sing in front of Imam [Khomeini.] We could sense the awkward and tense situation. We realized that music was controversial, and that performing under the circumstances could be even scandalous. I was certain that some audience members disapproved of the situation and considered it disgraceful. [In hindsight] our performance definitely served a hidden purpose and agenda. They [some authorities] wanted the nation to realize that Imam [Khomeini] has no problem with music, musical instruments, and music performance (Hosseini, 2016, 2:01:58).

The second instance of displaying musical instruments on IRIB Television occurred in December 1987 when the IRIB Sorud Centre produced a video series featuring orchestral music with mixed choir and male vocal soloists.[51] These programs were broadcasted during primetime, sparking fierce objections from thirty-six members of the Iranian Islamic Parliament, as well as

---

[51] You can watch the performance of one of the most famous pieces from this series, '*Ey Sārebān*,' at: https: //www.aparat.com/v/q581fx9

Ayatollah Gilani during Tehran's Friday prayer. Consequently, the program was canceled. Almost three decades later, in 2014, a morning program briefly showcased a live performance by a band for ten seconds, but the program's producer labeled it as a mistake. Many musicians have criticized this unjust ban on displaying musical instruments on IRIB Television. For instance, as reported by The Guardian in January 2014, "A group of young musicians from a band called *Pallett* made their own stand against the ban. When they were invited to perform on the IRIB, they decided to mime playing the musical instruments." Kalhor emphasizes, "[Censorship] is believed to be in the nature of revolution. The unfortunate matter is that it continued [for years]" (Hosseini, 2016, 1:56:46). Javid further explains:

> At the time, the directors [of IRIB and *Ershād*] did not have a solid management, leadership or strategy for music, which is the main reason why many musicians, some even supporters of the revolution, fled the country, became isolated, or hid in the shadows (ibid., 1:54:48).

Alizadeh finally returned to Iran after five years of exile and faced numerous obstacles from the authorities. Despite these challenges, he reunited with some former colleagues from the *Sheida and Aref Ensembles*, along with new members, and they successfully organized and performed the *Shurangiz* concert in October 1988. These concerts, held over six nights at *Vahdat*

Hall, marked a significant milestone as the first public concerts after the revolution. People traveled from various cities often spending the entire night outside the venue just to secure tickets for the concert the following night. Many came from different cities, braving the mid-autumn weather, equipped with thermoses and blankets to ensure a comfortable night's stay (Tasnim News Agency, 2019).

This event coincided with a series of mass executions of political prisoners ordered by Imam Khomeini, starting in July 1988 and continuing for several months. This deeply saddened performers, knowing some of their old mates might have been among those killed. Alizadeh recounts his memories of that event:

> It was not a concert. It was like a war. They [a group of the regime's armed forces] were in the hall, holding their firearms. I could see them sitting in the hall with their chins leaning on their gunstocks listening to the music. When I started performing, I kept pressing my toes on the floor to be sure that I still touched the stage. I am not exaggerating. It is not a fiction, a story, or a legend. I did feel weightless and a strange vertigo. However, my passion and enthusiasm to play the piece *Torkaman* at the end of my solo, motivated me to continue. I was playing *setār* with silent tears.[52] It was the greatest event and the

---

[52] *Setār* is an Iranian long-necked, plucked string instrument, with a small, pear-shaped sound box and four metal strings.

greatest joy of our [my and the music ensemble] lives (Hosseini, 2016, 2:05:03).

The post-war period saw a surge in musical activities, yet musicians encountered bureaucratic hurdles, requiring legal permits (mojavvez) even for minor events or projects. These permits were mandatory for various activities such as commercial music recordings, album productions, and both domestic and international concerts, all exclusively issued by the Ershād Sorud Centre (see Appendix G, Appendix H, and Appendix I). Musicians navigated complex procedures to obtain these permits, with control over music direction vested in committees within the Ershād Sorud Centre, comprising a select few musicians. However, this centralized control bred corruption, fostering favoritism that strained relations among musicians.

Over time, some musicians secured permits for Western classical, popular, and Persian traditional music (*musiqi-e asil-e Irani*) concerts, yet others, including electronic, hip-hop, and rock artists, often faced rejections. Consequently, many underground youth musicians turned to producing music at home and sharing it online as a workaround to circumvent these barriers, navigating the realm of music on the borderland.

PART II:

Micro Perspectives

Keyan's Journey: A Musical Odyssey Through Post-Revolutionary Iran

چون گفتنی باشد،
و همه عالم از ریش من در آویزد،
که مگر نگویم...،

اگرچه بعد از هزار سال باشد،
این سخن،
بدان کس برسد که من خواسته باشم!

شمس تبریزی، آیاتِ شمس (شماره ۷۸)

When words yearn to unfurl,
And all the world dangles from my beard,
To restrain me from saying...,

A time awaits, even if it spans a thousand years,
For these words
To reach the one for whom I yearn for.

Shams Tabrizi, Āyāt [Verses] (*No. 78*)

In a meeting with Dr. Niknafs, my doctoral research project supervisor at the University of Toronto, while discussing the narratives of Iranian composers, she made a brilliant suggestion: 'Why don't you tell your story as well?' She emphasized that as the author of this work, I should dedicate a section to recounting my personal, educational, and professional experiences. Upon reflection and revisiting my memories, I realized there were numerous untold stories. Unlike my family members, who diligently kept diaries and journals, I had never documented my life, feelings, experiences, or opinions. It was during this contemplation that I recalled Martin Scorsese's insightful remark: "The most personal is the most creative."

1. Revelation: The Wind of Change - First Brick in the Wall [53]

I was born in 1980 in Tehran, Iran—a child of the revolution, of fear, and of resilience—while my father was pursuing a Ph.D. in law in France. When I was a few months old, my mother and sister left me with my grandparents to join him in France. My mother had just secured a position as a physician in a hospital in Montpellier, Occitanie, when they decided to return. My parents chose to return out of fear for my father's

---

[53] The title "The Wind of Change - First Brick in the Wall" is inspired by the hit songs "Another Brick in the Wall" from the album "The Wall" by Pink Floyd and "Wind of Change" from the album "Crazy World" by Scorpions.

status in Iran. According to the new regime's ultimatum on the radio: retired army officers who had left the country were required to return immediately; otherwise, the government would identify them as fugitive officers and confiscate their pensions. Despite my father's reluctance, my mother insisted on returning.

My father, a colonel in the Shāh's army before the 1979 Revolution in Iran, requested early retirement at the age of forty-three immediately after the revolution in February 1979. He left Iran, likely seeking to recover from the trauma of drastic and sudden sociopolitical upheaval that profoundly altered his life. Upon his return to Iran, he found solace in music and sports, using them as a form of therapy.

2. Harmony: The Sound of Music[54]

One of my earliest childhood memories is of the night my father took me to *Edgaryan Piano Gallery*.[55] The place seemed like a wonderland to me. My father held my hand as we walked among pianos, the black and white keys gazing back at us. The vibrant sounds and sights of some intricately designed pianos overwhelmed my senses of vision and hearing. Despite the availability of cheaper options, my father chose to invest all our savings in buying the best one he could afford. The following

---

[54] The title "The Sound of Music" is a nod to the beloved musical drama film, a favorite of my father's.
[55] Hovick Edgaryan (1925–2016) was a musician, poet, and a violinist of the Tehran Symphony Orchestra. He established his piano company in 1945.

day, our new family member arrived: an upright mahogany Schimmel piano with built-in lamps on either side of the music stand, welcomed into our apartment in 1983.

My family discovered my passion for music during my childhood. It was evident when my parents observed my deep interest in music during visits to the house of Mr. J., a close friend and neighbor. I eagerly accompanied my father on these visits, drawn by Mr. J.'s stereo sound system and his collection of music records. Despite being a very active toddler, I would sit quietly next to the speakers, listening to music for hours. Additionally, I would often whistle the tunes and melodies that my elder sister played on the piano.

We lived on the third floor of a modest three-story building, with my grandparents residing on the first floor. One day, a neighbor from the second floor approached my mom, asking her, 'Could you please ask your husband to stop whistling in the early afternoon in the stairways? We usually nap at that time.' They found it hard to believe when my mother told them it was actually me who was whistling—a little boy's habit as I went down the stairs for lunch at my grandparents' apartment or returned upstairs to ours, happily whistling after a meal. I suppose I whistled too well, perhaps much louder than expected from a four-year-old boy.

3. Turmoil: The War (1980–1988) - Another Brick in the Wall (Part 1)

The eight-year war between Iran and Iraq left me with vivid memories, such as emergency population warnings during air raids on Tehran, war anthems, and giant X-shaped duct-tapes on glass doors and windows to prevent them from shattering due to the blast waves of bombs. The War of the Cities intensified and entered new, fiercer phases several years after the war broke out.[56] Initially, these air raids only occurred at night. When my parents returned home from work in the evening, we would drive to suburban areas in the east of Tehran, such as Jajrud, Bumehen, and Abali, seeking safety. During these drives, we listened to hits by pre-revolutionary Iranian pop singers, produced in Los Angeles and smuggled into Iran. I still remember my family's sing-along to Hassan Shamaizadeh's *'Bishtar O Bishtar'* chorus:

(هرچی ما میریم بیشتر و بیشتر، من دوستت دارم بیشتر و بیشتر)[57]
(The more and more we go, the more and more I love you)

On one occasion, we were driving to the eastern suburbs of Tehran on a winter evening, when all cars, driving to safety, got stuck in a gridlock. We turned off our engines upon hearing the

---

[56] The War of the Cities was five series of air raids, missile attacks and artillery shellings between 1984 to 1988 on major cities and urban areas, initiated by the Iraqi Air Force.
[57] Shamaizadeh. H. (1991). *Bishtar O Bishtar*. [Audio file]. https://open.spotify.com/track/5C0VuwUAPmjmYewpbFBkCN

emergency warning to helplessly and solemnly observe the confrontation of anti-aircraft weapons against Iraqi warplanes dropping bombs on Tehran. Eventually, after midnight, we all fell asleep inside our cars. It was only the next morning, when we woke up to a strong, disgusting odor and a view of Tehran's landfill, that we realized we had spent the night in a dump site. As residents returning from the suburb, we found ourselves stuck in unmoving traffic. My sister, who had an exam at school, was particularly anxious, so my mother and sister walked for a few kilometers until they reached another road and hitchhiked to Tehran in the back end of a pickup truck, standing or sitting in the cargo bed filled with tens of people desperate to get to the city.

Amidst this turmoil, the darkness cast its shadow over everything. When the emergency alert sounded, we had to quickly extinguish all the lights and take shelter in our basements. In second grade, I attended another school during the early evenings in November due to the temporary closure of my elementary school. As a young child, I found it disheartening to go to school in the late afternoon. Additionally, we experienced daily blackouts lasting three hours in all districts of Tehran, especially during peak times. Although the newspapers published weekly power outage schedules for different districts in advance, more often than not, the outages did not adhere to the timetable.

When the air strikes intensified, my parents decided to spend weekends in the suburbs. We visited safer areas like

Kilavand, Damavand, or Karaj to stay with relatives. My aunt and uncle owned a cottage in Karaj-Hesarak, where we frequently spent weekends. One day, my father, my uncle, and I went onto the roof to adjust the antenna for television reception. I was shocked to see an Iraqi bomber flying very close to us at low altitude, below Iranian air radars to evade detection. While my father and uncle joked about it, their humor couldn't distract me; witnessing that scene filled me with horror.

As Iraqi air strikes became more frequent and sudden, and with no emergency population alert to provide time for shelter, my father decided to install metal frame beds in the underground parking lot of my mother's private medical clinic. We relocated to the safe underground parking area and remained there during those uncertain times, allowing my mother to continue working and us to pursue our education. Some of our friends, relatives, and other residents of the building joined us in that parking facility. Many nights, we gathered together in the underground parking on level three, with someone playing the guitar and others singing along. While the regime beat the drums of war above ground, we found solace in coming together to sing during those gloomy nights, helping us overcome the trauma of war night after night and week after week.

Years later, the term 'underground music' became a trend in Iran. This term refers to youth creating popular music in Iran, including Rock and Hip-Hop (Nooshin, 2005). Regardless of what it means in Iran or in general, this term evokes memories of those moments I spent *zir-e-zamin*, in the underground parking lot full of cockroaches, listening to live music performance, while playing hide and seek with other children in the semi-darkness.[58] The foreground sounds of children, blended with the middle ground sound of adults singing *Qoqāye Setāregān*, as well as the background sound of bombs and emergency warnings, will forever remain in my mind as the definition of Iran's underground music.[59]

Since my parents heard that the Iraqi air force would not attack Qom, the religious capital of Iran, we visited this city during Nowruz in 1987. I didn't feel excited when I heard of my parents' decision because I thought we would have to spend all our time praying while staying there. Interestingly, my experience contradicted my preconceived notions and mental image of Qom; our relatives, who owned mosques and hotels for Qom's pilgrims, did not practice religion at home. They had VCRs, so we enjoyed watching many uncensored Western and Indian movies, which were illegal at the time and smuggled into the country, including 'First Blood' and 'Sholay,' the most famous movies of that time in Iran.[60] As a result of that trip my image of Qom shifted from the Vatican of Iran to something closer to the Vegas of Iran. During our evening gatherings, my extended maternal family of over thirty people were all making

---

[58] '*Zir-e-zamin*' is the Persian term for underground.
[59] Khorram H. (1986). *Qoqāye Setāregān*. Parvin. [Audio file]. https://open.spotify.com/track/7j4VgS6jbtxANMAQogYtJb?si=0JhLLdTyQB CCduU-2IpRzg
[60] Sholay is a 1975 Indian action-adventure film.

fun of the regime's heads, by imitating their voices while wearing a cloak and a turban. Then, men played Poker, Rummy or Blackjack, and women danced, played *dāyere*, and sang:[61]

آی انار انار بیا به بالینم

آی در شب تار بیا به بالینم[62]

Hey pomegranate (playful beloved girl), come to my bedside
Hey come to my bedside in this dark and dreary night

I still vividly remember that winter night of 1988. Iraq had announced that their air forces would attack Tehran. Horrified, I asked my father, 'Dad, let's shelter in the underground parking.' He reassured me, 'No worries, Yankee,' one of his nicknames for me. 'During heavy rains and stormy weather, bombers cannot fly over Tehran's sky.' He added, 'We don't need to go there; we're safe at home.'

In the middle of the night, an emergency warning sounded; he was surprised, and we went down to the basement of our building. It scared me, but my father believed it could be a false alarm. After several minutes, we returned to our apartment to sleep.

A little later, before we could go back to sleep, the second emergency warning began. We jumped up and ran down as fast as we could. I insisted on going to the underground shelter at

---

[61] *Dāyere* is a Persian medium-sized frame drum with jingles.
[62] Lyra Entertainment. (2021, April 30). *Anar Anar* [Video file]. Retrieved from https://www.youtube.com/watch?v=lbFy9hmOi2M

my mother's clinic, but my parents calmed me down. They decided to stay in the TV room of my grandparents' apartment on the ground floor.

I still recall that dreadful night. I tried to sleep on a mattress on the floor, but I couldn't, as the dreadful image of big bombs falling on our home haunted my mind. Contrary to my father's prediction, the Iraqis attacked seven times that night. They dropped no bombs, exactly as he predicted, but they sent a different gift to us: al-Husayn missiles.[63]

Once the missile attacks escalated, many civilians in Tehran decided to leave the city (Tyler, 1988). This included my parents. My uncle owned a villa in Daryā Kenār, one of the resort cities on the southern coast of the Caspian Sea, where we stayed for several months. I enjoyed swimming in the sea, playing on the sandy beach, and gaming on my home pong telegame console connected to a portable five-inch black and white television.

However, I still remember my concern for my uncle, a very wealthy ophthalmologist, as I overheard him speaking with my father, 'I do not know how to survive if this situation continues for one more week.' At the time, many could not even imagine an end to the grueling war. The regime's propaganda

---

[63] Al Hussein is the designation of an Iraqi short-range ballistic missile. The missile was the result of upgrading the Soviet made Scud in order to achieve a longer range. The weapon was widely used by the Iraqi Army during the Iran–Iraq War. Up to two hundred missiles were launched against Iran between 1987 and 1988, killing some two thousand people. Tehran, Qom, and Isfahan became the usual targets. Their poor accuracy, while mostly ineffective to conduct a major strategic campaign, made them basically weapons of terror, forcing thousands of refugees out of the main Iranian cities.

portrayed it as a divine test of the Muslim's faith, a spiritual war of righteousness against evil to its ultimate elimination. Therefore, Imam Khomeini's historical statement shocked the nation when he stated:

> Up until a few days ago, I believed in our previously-stated position and defense strategy towards war, convinced that it benefited our system, revolution and country. However, recent events and undisclosed factors led me to accept the resolution. God willing, these factors will become clear in the future. Taking this decision was more deadly than taking poison. I submitted myself to God's will and drank this drink [poison] for his satisfaction. (Pear & Times, 1988, paras. 3–8)

Eventually, after one year of rejecting all attempts to end the war and just two weeks after the US Navy shot down Iran Air Passenger Flight 655, the Iranian government signed the immediate ceasefire, United Nations Security Council Resolution 598.

4. Uncertainty: Postwar Music Education

After the war, many individuals sought music lessons, leading to the establishment of music programs in private institutes across Tehran. Despite this demand, some of these classes operated discreetly and cautiously. One of my former piano students described his first lessons, portraying the atmosphere of those days. He recounts, 'I felt so excited when I got admitted to Tehran Polytechnic University in 1988.'[64] Not only was he starting his undergraduate studies in one of Iran's most prestigious universities but he also did not need to fear the compulsory military recruitment anymore. He continues:

> My father gave me an electric keyboard as a gift to celebrate my achievement, so I began searching for piano lessons. When I found a music class near the Polytechnic University, I eagerly anticipated starting my long-time dream of learning to play the piano. However, upon arriving for my first lesson, the shabby building, which seemed suitable for all sorts of illegal activities except music lessons, shocked me. Climbing the stairs to the music studio located on the third level, I noticed there was no sign on the door. After knocking several times, someone finally opened the door, cautiously checking the surroundings before letting me in. This suspicious behavior made me very uncomfortable and eventually developed into a phobia. I began to worry about what might happen if authorities stormed into the studio during

---

[64] Tehran Polytechnic University was founded in 1928 as a standard academy, developed into the university of technology by Habib Nafisi in 1956, and has consistently been ranked as one of Iran's top universities. National university entrance exams are competitive and stressful. Hundreds of thousands of candidates are ranked according to their grades, and a student needs to be among the top one percent to be admitted to the top universities.

a piano lesson and arrested us all. Consequently, after just a couple of lessons, I decided to quit. I wanted to enjoy playing my favorite songs without causing trouble for myself and my family.

As a result, and under the very specific circumstances of high uncertainty about the government's policy on music education, private tutors mostly offered music lessons at home (see Appendix J). When I turned eight, I began private lessons at home instead of taking lessons in music institutions or conservatories. In contrast to the unpleasant experience of my student, I enjoyed playing the études in *Beyer's Elementary Piano Method, Op. 101*.

My first piano instructor rarely played the pieces himself, nor did he explain any aspects of piano performance. However, I consider him my role model for two reasons: Firstly, it took him at least ten minutes to climb three flights of stairs to reach our apartment on the third floor, and almost the same amount of time to descend the stairs carefully after each lesson to reach his car. I could feel every single step my mobility-challenged piano teacher took to navigate the steep stairways. I have always admired his hard work and resilience as a music educator.

Secondly, on the very last day, he asked my father to hire another piano teacher. My father wondered whether I had misbehaved or neglected to practice. He asked my piano teacher about my progress during lessons, and why he recommended another teacher. The teacher replied, 'I can assure you of your son's brilliance. However, I cannot offer him any more materials, sir.' To this day, I do not know the real reason, but I must admit that his response was the most humble and sincere I have ever heard.

Later on, during my music education journey, I learned a lot from different music teachers. Nonetheless, I consider myself fortunate to have started my music journey with such an admirable individual. His strong positive influence has formed my first impression of music teachers as very respectful and honorable people, which eventually (and perhaps unconsciously) led me to follow in his footsteps years later.

5. Dissonance: Lost (1992) - Another Brick in the Wall (Part 2)

"Trigger Warning: Extremely violent and graphic descriptions ahead"

One of our neighbors, Mr. J., an Assyrian man, worked for an airline at the airport.[65] He lived alone after his family immigrated to the United States in 1979 during the revolution. J., a very sociable person with many friends, received visitors frequently, especially because of his access to alcoholic beverages—strictly prohibited in Iran after the 1979 Revolution—as a non-Muslim person. He made friends with a

---

[65] The Assyrians are a people who have lived in the Middle East since ancient times and today can be found all over the world.

Pāsdār—a member of *Sepāh* (I guess a junior member). Soon, they became close friends, which led to J. calling him '*Dādāš*' ['brother']. After a while, J. disappeared. His wife and daughter came to Iran to find him. Because of our family's friendship with J. and his family, my parents and I—barely twelve years old at the time—went to their home to welcome them. J.'s daughter went to the kitchen to get something to eat from the fridge as his wife was talking to my parents, "I wonder why he bought and froze so much meat in the fridge before disappearing." The rest looks like a horror movie. His wife had not finished her sentence when his daughter returned to the living room, with a plastic bag in her hand, threw the bag in the living room, and shrieked, "This is his head, in the fridge, this is his head."

My mother grabbed me and ran back to our home, while my father stayed with the shocked family of the victim. To make this even more horrific, they later realized that the frozen meat in the freezer was the unfortunate man's flesh, as his murderers butchered him after tying him to a chair at his kitchen table and strangling him to death.

Later, investigations revealed that '*Dādāš*' with his two accomplices (one of them a butcher), forced J. to sign a document transferring his two storey house to '*Dādāš*'. Then, they killed him, mutilated his lifeless body, flushed some of his flesh down the toilet, threw away some in a remote area, and cold-bloodedly bagged and stored the remaining in the victim's own freezer. Surprisingly, these men did not receive a fitting punishment, except for maybe some time in jail. Under Islamic Penal Code of Iran, Muslims murdering non-Muslims incur a penalty, but they do not receive retaliatory punishment (Ghazi, 2019).

I personally remember J. because he invited me to listen to some of the best music that he owned. My father turned to music to heal from the trauma of the revolution in Iran after he returned from France in 1980. Similarly, to help his young son recover from the trauma of witnessing a horrific scene, he encouraged me to turn to music too. This time, he bought me a Casio CT-670 keyboard in 1992 and put it in my room. I used to play only piano pieces and études as part of my music homework on our Schimmel upright piano before having the electric keyboard. The Casio keyboard unlocked my inner musician. For the first time, I really enjoyed mixing the preset tones and rhythms, improvising my own tunes, and searching to find proper chords to harmonize my melodies. Playing my own songs on that keyboard helped me overcome this trauma and broadened my horizons.

Furthermore, my father enrolled me in weekly piano lessons at *Kanoon-e Musiqi-e Chang* music institution, recommended by our neighbor, whose daughter took music lessons there with Mr. Hosseini. (see Appendix K). Instead of registering me in his class, my father registered me with another piano teacher, one of the students of maestro Emanuel Melik

Aslanian.[66] One day, my piano teacher couldn't make it to class. Mr. Kamian, the owner and founder of Chang, substituted for my private lesson. For the first time, a piano teacher praised my performance with a kind attitude and asked why I was taking piano lessons. I replied that I really liked it. He said, "Good to hear, but still not enough. You have to love music." As a young teenage boy, I found this to be strange advice. Today, after many years, I regard his statement as one of the most remarkable pieces of advice I have ever heard. One will thrive, fulfill an obligation, and find meaning only in the loving pursuit of a purpose. Otherwise, they will perish and surrender in the face of all hindrances and obstacles. As Hafez famously said centuries ago:[67]

از صدای سخن عشق ندیدم خوشتر
یادگاری که در این گنبد دوار بماند

None sweeter than love's voice, I've found
A cherished keepsake in the revolving dome's bound

A few weeks later, he suggested to my father that I join *Chang Youth Orchestra* for the twenty-second anniversary of *Chang*. It was the first time I had the opportunity to perform on piano in a mixed ensemble. The ensemble included a male Iranian traditional singer, two violins, two *santurs*, two *setārs*, piano,

---

[66] Emanuel Melik Aslanian (1915–2003) was one of the greatest Iranian-Armenian pianists and composers of Iran.
[67] Hafez (1315-1390): Renowned Persian poet known for his lyrical poetry on love and spirituality. His "Divan of Hafez" is a cornerstone of Persian literature.

and *tombak*.[68] Rehearsals taught me that playing Persian traditional pieces on piano as part of a mixed ensemble can be more enjoyable than I had anticipated. This experience contradicted the opinions of some Iranian musicians who believed in drawing a strict line between Western and Persian traditional music (*musiqi-e asil-e Irani*) and musical instruments. Some even argued for the superiority of one genre over the other or insisted that each genre should be played with its corresponding instruments. I still vividly remember the piano parts and the two songs, 'Remember Me' (*Be Yād-e Man Bāš*) and 'Butterfly Ashes' (*Xākestar-e Parvāne*), both composed by Mr. Kamian.

Today, nearly thirty years later, I believe Mr. Kamian, an Iranian musician and music teacher, intentionally composed those pieces to impart a valuable lesson to his young students: music serves as a bridge that connects people, nations, and generations. Decades later, I encountered a similar approach in the documentary *East Jerusalem/West Jerusalem*.[69] Despite Jerusalem's long standing division, spanning over half a century, the documentary showcases how David Broza, a Palestinian singer-songwriter, collaborated with Israeli and Arab musicians to create and perform music on the borderland. Their aim was to convey a message of peace and solidarity to the world.

---

[68] *Santur* is a Persian hammer dulcimer. *Tonbak* is a Persian skin-covered goblet drum played with bare hands.
[69] *East Jerusalem/West Jerusalem* (2014) is a documentary film directed by Henrique Cymerman and Erez Miller.

However, not all musicians and teachers shared the same perspective. Before my piano lessons at *Chang*, I used to practice my études and pieces in a practice room. On one occasion, while rehearsing the two Persian traditional songs to prepare for the ensemble, my piano teacher burst into the room and angrily demanded to know what I was playing. Startled, I explained that I was practicing for the upcoming students' concert. She then demanded to know who permitted me to play such music. I replied that it was Mr. Kamian, the school director, who invited me to join the Persian ensemble. She vehemently insisted that her students should only play Western classical music. Faced with this rigid attitude, I made the decision to continue my music lessons with a different teacher—one who possessed a more open mind, was more encouraging, and inspired me further.

My new teacher introduced a practice that had a profound impact on my future. At the conclusion of each piano lesson, I was instructed to transcribe only the melody of the piece into my notebook from my teacher's original piano sheet. Then, I was tasked with discovering the accompanying chords at home. After notating them, I would double-check with him during the following session. I found immense joy in this process and relished the practice. It afforded me the opportunity to learn popular songs while infusing them with my own harmonies. Consequently, my lessons became more vibrant and dynamic compared to my previous piano instruction, which primarily focused on the rigid repetition of conventional piano method books such as Beyer, Czerny, and Hanon.

In the early 1990s, obtaining sheet music in Iran remained a challenge. Despite Tehran's population of over six million at the time, the city hosted very few music stores. One such establishment was *Eskandarian*, a renowned music bookstore located in downtown Tehran. I vividly recall that they did not display any sheet music previews in the showroom. Instead, they would take orders and retreat to another room at the back of the store to photocopy sheet music for customers. On occasion, they would ask us to return the following day to collect our orders. Furthermore, they charged a high price for material of poor quality.

After the war, Iran's economy started to recover (Mojaver, 2009), leading to a relaxation of the previously stringent social and business norms. People began to earn and spend more money, particularly on their children's education. This period also saw the establishment of private non-profit schools, which aimed to enhance students' opportunities to succeed in the highly competitive university entrance exams.

The most popular private schools admitted a selected group of students with the highest GPA scores. However, having a high GPA did not guarantee admission. Ideological interviews (*Gozinesh*) became a part of the school admissions process (Rahimi, 2015). In fact, students and their families had to undergo separate *Gozinesh* interviews, which included questions about their interests in different recreational programs, religious beliefs and practices, and the family's history of sociopolitical activism. To maximize their children's chances of admission to certain religious schools, mothers had to wear '*chādor*', a traditional Islamic garment that covers the body, and both parents and children had to remain discreet about their interests and activities outside of school.

My first year of high school coincided with the opening of non-profit schools for the first time after the revolution. My family prioritized education, so they embarked on a quest to enroll me in the most prestigious and popular high school they could find. The schools invited us to many interviews and asked a variety of bizarre questions to which we did not know the "right" answer, such as "Do you watch the Miss Marple television series on IRIB Television? (Yes or No and why)" and "Does your child have his or her own room in the house?" Despite my excellent GPA, I was not granted admission to almost any popular public schools due to my parents' "poor" performance at the interviews.

Finally, my parents ended up enrolling me in one of the best private schools. After reviewing my GPA, the school's admission office contacted us and invited my parents for an interview. Overwhelmed by pressure and guilt, my parents tried their best to seize this opportunity. My mother wore the '*chādor*' as a sign of respect to the Islamic ideology and attended the interview with my father to increase my chances.

Similar to previous interviews, this one also became another arduous session of irrelevant questions, mainly about our family background and ideological views. The interviewer stated that the interview had ended and he did not see a chance. However, the real interview started when my father spoke out:

>-You asked us so many questions, sir. Would you mind me asking you just one question?
>-Not at all, please.
>-All I know about you is your last name, which reminds me of a very old and dear friend, Mr. E., an officer of gendarmerie[70] in Fasā (an Iranian city). Are you by any chance related to him?

Surprised, he answered:

>-Of course, he is my uncle.
>-It's my pleasure to meet you. Your uncle was actually one of my officers and friends.

The interviewer, Mr. E., then nodded to my father with a knowing look and a hand gesture indicating that his uncle used to drink vodka shots.[71] He said: "Sir, why did you waste so much of my time? We just wanted to make sure we did not register the children of dogmatic religious families here at a

---

[70] Gendarmerie: The Iranian Gendarmerie, initially a rural police force, later became a modern highway patrol. Established in 1910 during the Qajar era, it held political influence until the end of the Pahlavi era, when it was modernized into the Imperial Iranian Gendarmerie.
[71] A very popular alcoholic drink in Iran, a.k.a. *araq sagi*.

school where my son and my friends' sons study. We will offer you a great discount, the absolute minimum registration fee. Your son is welcome."

Similar to the other high schools, this one held religious ceremonies, including the mandatory daily Congregational Prayer and weekly *Ziyārat Āšurā* on Thursdays.[72] However, beneath the surface, students were engaged in exchanging illegal music cassettes and video tapes. Within my circle of classmates and with the availability of (illegal) satellite dishes, I had the opportunity to listen to some of the best rock bands for the first time, including Nirvana, Queen, Dire Straits, Aerosmith, Guns N' Roses, and Scorpions. We also exchanged our parents' music archives, which included The Beatles, The Doors, Pink Floyd, Led Zeppelin, Jimi Hendrix and many more.

It seems that fear replaced genuine respect in schools at that time. All students were required to stand up when teachers entered the classroom, and failure to do so was seen as an act of irreverence and disrespect by the teachers. However, I believe that in some cases, students stood up not out of genuine respect, but rather out of fear. I remember one of my professors at the University of Toronto told me that he found it funny when one of the new Iranian doctoral students, sitting at the other end of the lobby, stood up when he walked past on the other side and

---

[72] Congregational Prayer is held in congregation and is among the important acts of worship in Islam. *Ziyarat Āšurā* is a Shia salutatory prayer to Husayn ibn Ali and the martyrs of the *Battle of Karbala*.

then sat again after greetings. I mentioned to him that she did it as a token of respect in Persian culture.

6. Quest: In Search of Lost Time

After graduation from the Tehran Polytechnic University, I had no plans to pursue further education and started working as a Quality Assurance Engineer Supervisor at a company providing automative paints for *Iran Khodro*.[73] After a couple of months, I realized that this job was consuming all my time and energy. I expressed my concerns to my mom, admitting that if I continued this way, my life would be unfulfilling, as I couldn't pursue my dream of becoming a musician while working from 6 am to 6 pm and having no energy left afterward.

However, an unexpected incident changed my course. While browsing through my sister's pamphlet for a Master's program application, I stumbled upon a surprising detail: applicants were allowed to apply for a Master's program unrelated to their bachelor's degree, a first in Iran. Curious about this opportunity, I discussed it with Mr. Dibazar, the former dean of the Faculty of Music at Tehran University of Art, during my very first music lesson. He confirmed the validity of the information and encouraged me to consider a

---

[73] Iran Khodro, established in 1962, is the largest automaker in Iran. It produces a diverse range of vehicles, including passenger cars, commercial vehicles, and buses, and holds partnerships with international automotive brands.

Master's degree in composition as a potential career path in music. Despite his encouragement, I felt uncertain. At twenty-two, I feared it might be too late and unwise to abandon a secure engineering career for a new profession as a composer. Lacking the courage for such a life-altering decision, I initially declined to continue my music lessons. However, a few months later, I mustered the courage to reconsider. I resumed my lessons with Mr. Dibazar, applied for a Master's degree in Music Composition, passed the entrance exam, and was admitted with the highest score.

A few years later, my thesis defense took place in the main amphitheater of the Faculty of Music at *Dānešgāh-e Honar,* with many students and guests in attendance. After the performance of my piece, the very first comment from one of the committee members was, 'Congratulations Keyan, your piece completely reflects your inner voice and passionate personality. However, I think your three-movement symphony carries political undertones.' Opting not to respond or acknowledge his comment, I remained silent. He then proceeded to inquire further about my piece. Rather than discussing the underlying message I intended to convey through my work, I focused solely on its technical aspects.

During my thesis defense, which was open to the public, I harbored concerns that a representative of the Ministry of Intelligence might be among the audience members. In Iran, security offices (*Herāsat*) are present in all universities and public organizations. The *Herāsat* videographer recorded my defense session, intensifying my worry that officials could potentially gain access to it.

Interestingly, a few minutes later, one of the committee members asked the videographer to halt recording before recounting his memories of music from the Shāh's era, pre-revolution. For reasons unknown to me, even after so many years, I did not ask the videographer to stop recording my session so that I could speak freely about my work.

Even when prompted by jury members about the reason for the incorporation of a very famous revolutionary song—*Yār-e Dabestāni-e Man* [My Elementary School Friend]—into my piece as one of the main motifs, I refrained from divulging the intended message. I still maintain that my symphony lacks any political agenda, yet in a repressive society devoid of free speech, everything can be viewed through a political lens.

Years later, I discovered that my sister had also utilized this controversial revolutionary song in a play she wrote and directed during her middle school years in the mid-1980s.

7. Solidarity: A Composer's Tribute to Loss - Another Brick in the Wall (Part 3)

Ms. Ebadi, I will always remember your words: 'You are so lucky; as a composer, you can work in your cozy private studio and enjoy your life forever.'[74] You were the only one who foresaw this possibility, and that vision became a reality. After listening to my master's dissertation for thirty-two minutes, you honored me by requesting a piece of music for your worthy peace campaign. Your approval and affirmation meant a great deal to me, but regrettably, I did not fulfill your request. I am sorry for this decision, driven by fear for my future. I was concerned that it might jeopardize my career as a lecturer at the Tehran University of Art. Sadly, many of my colleagues share similar fears for their jobs, families, loved ones, and lives. In our reality, those who dare to exercise their right to freedom of speech often pay a heavy price, sometimes with their lives.

Twelve years later and thousands of miles away, in Toronto, Canada, I felt the first surge of composer's pride as my piece found its noble purpose. In that moment, unity and solidarity echoed through my work, resonating with our shared quest for peace.

Composition of "Reera" predates the tragic downing of Flight PS752.[75] In 2016, *Sarv Choir* commissioned me to

---

[74] Shirin Ebadi (born 1947) is an Iranian Nobel Peace Prize laureate, lawyer, and former judge known for her advocacy of human rights, particularly focusing on the rights of women, children, and political prisoners in Iran.

[75] Ukraine Flight PS752: The passenger plane crash in Iran resulted in the loss of all 176 people on board. *Sepāh*, an Iranian military organization, shot down the aircraft on January 8, 2020. Initially, Iranian aviation authorities denied the missile strike, attributing the incident to a technical error. Conversely, Ukrainian authorities, after initially accepting Iran's explanation, later considered a shoot-down as one of their primary theories. Subsequent investigations by Western intelligence agencies and the public confirmed that the aircraft was indeed downed by Iranian-launched missiles. Three days later, on January 11, *Sepāh* acknowledged responsibility for the incident, citing a case

compose a choral piece inspired by 'Reera,' one of the most famous poems by the modern Persian poet Nima Yushij. In this poem, the poet perceives a faint sound echoing from the woods, resembling a human voice, only to realize it's not human but perhaps Reera herself, yearning to sing in the dark night but silenced by her departed voice. I intertwined lines from Yannis Ritsos's poetry about peace, such as "Peace is a child's sleep," into this composition.

After three years, my piece finally premiered on December 14th, 2019. This performance coincided with the tragic downing of Flight 752 in Iran, resulting in the loss of all passengers, including Reera Esmaeilion, a nine-year-old girl, and her mother, who lived in Toronto. Consequently, I renamed this piece 'Elegy for Reera', published the video on YouTube, and dedicated it to Reera and all the victims of the Iran plane crash.[76] My piece provided solace to those affected by the incident, offering them a sense of being heard and respected. I felt deeply honored when the Esmailion family requested its performance at the memorial ceremony for their beloved family members, Reera and Parisa, held on February 2nd, 2020. Ms. Ebadi, today, I believe in destiny, in kismet, and in the inevitability of our fates.

---

of mistaken identity where they targeted the plane, believing it to be a cruise missile.
[76] Keyan Emami. (2020, January 12). "Elegy for Reera"–To Reera and All the Victims of the Iran Plane Crash [Video file]. https://youtu.be/Ch7-WULZ2eo

Coda: The Post-Revolution Musical Landscape

When someone mentions war in Iran, the immediate association is often with the long and grueling Iran-Iraq war. However, there was another exhausting conflict silently raging within the depths of Iranian music society during the 1980s, mirroring the Iran-Iraq war.

The Iranian government banned music immediately after the 1979 Revolution, marginalizing and dismissing many eminent musicians. *Motrebi* music was declared *harām* (forbidden by Islamic law), and the performance of other genres such as pop, classical, opera, and ballet was also prohibited. Musicians were required to obtain a permit to carry their instruments, and centers of music education ceased their activities for several years. As a result, most musicians and music teachers could only conduct lessons in private residences. Additionally, an unwritten decree prohibited IRIB (*Sedā o Simā*) Television from featuring musical instruments in its programs.

Soon, the Iranian government realized that they could not completely eliminate the music. They needed some form of music not only for the media but also to advance the regime's propaganda. To make it acceptable to hard-liners with a strong bias against music, authorities abolished prevailing, well-established music terms and created new terminology.

Furthermore, they outlined guidelines—sometimes clear, but often vague—to define and authorize their own 'brand' of music that did not violate Islamic law. IRIB commissioned *soruds*, the rebranded and dictated form of music, to glorify the war and martyrdom.

Even though many rules and regulations changed fundamentally, for many aspects of life and society, change remained superficial. Despite the ban on music, music enthusiasts continued to listen, and musicians continued to compose. Instead, a form of resistance emerged, where people created, performed, and listened to music in the privacy of their homes. Recordings, and sometimes even musical instruments, were smuggled into the country and sold stealthily.

The impact of this exhausting conflict was also felt by individual musicians, who faced the difficult decision of whether to remain in Iran despite restrictions or immigrate elsewhere. Some professional musicians chose exile and contributed to the creation of *Tehrangelesi* pop music, a distinctive genre of post-revolutionary pop music that emerged in Los Angeles (Hemmasi, 2020). Others opted to stay in Iran and played a role in reopening music conservatories and universities six years after the revolution in 1984. In the following years, some musicians even managed to obtain legal permits for organizing music concerts.

Meanwhile, a new generation of highly determined and resilient Iranian-born musicians, who are currently active all around the world, was nurtured. Similarly, when faced with many dilemmas, I had to choose: whether to pursue my dream of becoming a professional musician or to abandon it. Ultimately, I decided to dedicate myself to the world of music. I was among the flock of phoenixes that rose from the ashes and soared high, educating, performing, studying, and composing music on the borderland.

Postlude: A Celebration of Rebirth

Bābā! Do you know how I feel now after sharing our story? A sense of relief washes over me, like experiencing a spiritual rebirth. *Bābā*, how could you leave us on the very same day you were born? After your passing, your sister shared some beautiful memories of you. She mentioned how, when you were young, you delighted in dancing to your favorite songs by Mireille Mathieu, Edith Piaf, and Dalida. You were brimming with life and cherished peace, joy, and music.

Bābā, when you retired from the armed forces right after the revolution, you spent many years supporting our hard-working mom in establishing her medical clinic. She told me how diligently you learned and worked to build and manage that private clinic. Though you never returned to that line of duty, you fought alongside our mother to bring joy, peace, and love into our family, infusing music into our lives.

Bābā, your compassion knew no bounds. You couldn't stand dishonesty or injustice, and you couldn't bear to see anyone in distress. Are you now solemnly observing the Iranian doctors and nurses bravely battling COVID-19 on the front lines, armed with nothing but their dedication, resilience, and determination? Have you heard that we've lost many of them in this fight? Does it not remind you of the Iran-Iraq war, when *Sepāh* commanders callously used defenseless, sometimes child soldiers as human shields on the landmines during the eight years of warfare?

Bābā, have you seen the healthcare workers in Iran dancing together in their protective medical gear? Shall we dance in their honor? I "Wish You Were Here" to dance to your all-time favorite "The Sound of Music" with these "Sultans of Swing."[77]

Like the good old days, I wish I could wake up to your music every morning once again—to the melodies you played on your violin. Perhaps when our story reaches its end, our dreams will come true, and you'll join us from the underground so we can dance freely and joyfully together aboveground, celebrating our rebirth, a celebration for all humankind.

---

[77] "Wish You Were Here" by Pink Floyd and "Sultans of Swing" by Dire Straits are the titles of two of my favorite tracks.

Epilogue

بنمای رخ که باغ و گلستانم آرزوست   بگشای لب که قند فراوانم آرزوست
ای آفتاب حُسن برون آ دمی ز ابر   کآن چهرهٔ مُشَعشَعِ تابانم آرزوست
جانم ملول گشت ز فرعون و ظلم او   آن نور روی موسی عمرانم آرزوست
یک دست جام باده و یک دست جعد یار   رقصی چنین میانه میدانم آرزوست
باقی این غزل را ای مطرب ظریف   زین سان همی‌شمار که زین سانم آرزوست

مولوی، غزل شماره ۴۴۱

Reveal your countenance, for I long for the orchard and rose garden,
Part your lips, for I yearn for abundant sugar.
O sun of beauty, emerge for a moment from behind the cloud,
For I long for that radiant, shining face.
My spirit languishes from Pharaoh and his tyranny,
I yearn for the radiant visage of Moses, the son of Imran.
With a goblet of wine in one hand and the beloved's curl in the other,
I yearn for such a dance at the centre of the stage.
Cunning troubadour, coninue this ode in a similar fashion,
For 'tis the fashion for which I yearn.

Rumi, Ghazal No. 441[78]

---

[78] Rumi (1207–1273) was a Persian poet and sufi.

Appendices

Appendix A

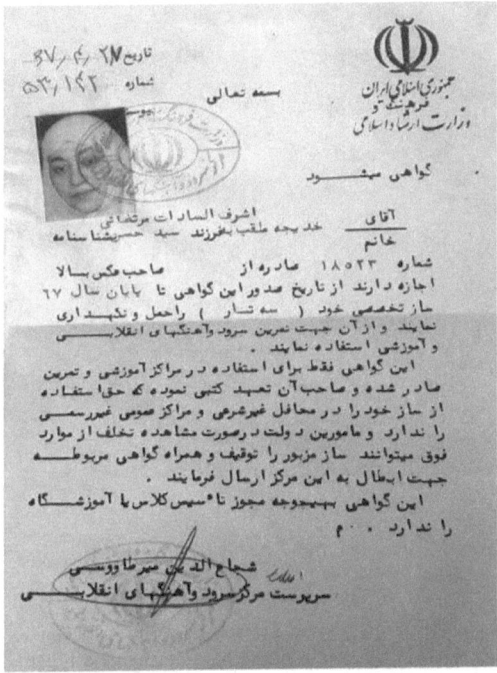

Figure 1 Marzieh's one-year permit (*mojavvez*) to carry her *setār* (1988)[79]

Marzieh's one-year permit grants her permission to carry her musical instrument, the *setār*, for the purpose of practicing sorud and revolutionary songs, as well as teaching these types of music. However, the permit restricts the use of her instrument to educational settings only; it explicitly prohibits its use in public or at gatherings contrary to Sharia standard. Breaching this condition may result in seizure of both the instrument and the permit by authorities. Additionally, the permit prohibits Marzieh from opening a music academy under its authorization. (Appendix figure for page 33)

---

[79] Marziyeh—born Ashraf o-Sadat Mortezaie—(1924–2010) was an Iranian singer of Persian traditional music (*musiqi-e asil-e Irani*).

Appendix B

Figure 2 Broken Vinyl: Legacy of Revolution

One of the Earliest 10" Records in Iran, Exclusive to the IRIB Archive, recorded by the Gramophone Company in early 1906 (catalog no. 4-12016). Featuring musicians Ghorban Khan, Mirza Mohammed Khan, and Ismail Khan, it was released under the Gramophone label with the "Recording Angel" trademark.

Source: Kazemi, Pour Ahmad, Farahani. (2011). Call of Honor. Tehran: Iranian Academy of the Arts, p. 217. (Appendix figure for page 40)

Appendix C

Figure 3 Broken Vinyl: Legacy of Revolution

One of the early recordings featuring Iranian female singer Ghamar El-Moulouk Waziri, catalog no. 7-213462, from the IRIB Archive. Recorded by the Gramophone Company in early 1926 and released under the His Master's Voice label, with musician Mortaza Khan Ney Davoud.

Source: Kinnear, Michael. (2019). The Gramophone Company's Persian Recordings 1899 to 1934. Australia: Bajakhana, p. 90. (Appendix figure for page 40)

Appendix D

Figure 4 Ershād Letter: 1979 Revolution Anniversary Performance (1986)

Letter from the head of Ershād Sorud Centre regarding students' performance at the 1986 anniversary ceremony of the 1979 Revolution, featuring students from Sorud and Revolutionary Songs Conservatory–Boys and Girls Centers.

Source: National Archives of Iran[80] – Document No: 4686157. (Appendix figure for page 44)

---

[80] The National Archives of Iran (*Sāzmān-e Asnād-e Iran*) is Iran's largest research center, situated in Haqqani and Mirdamad in Tehran.

Appendices 101

Appendix E

Figure 5 Musicians in Military Attire Performing Before Officials During Iran-Iraq War

Photo of Wind and Percussion Band and Men's Choir performance in the 1980s. (Appendix figure for page 51)

Appendix F

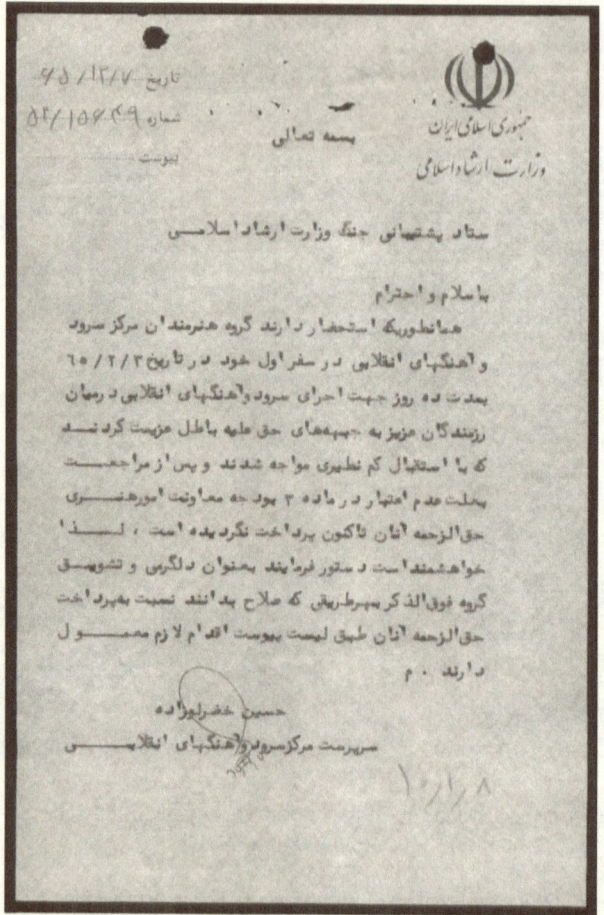

Figure 6 Ershād Letter: Compensation for Musicians Assigned to War Zones (1987)

Follow-up letter requesting compensation from Ershād's Supportive Council of War Department for musicians' 10-day performance in a war zone (1987).

Source: National Archives of Iran – Document No: 4673644. (Appendix figure for page 51)

Appendix G

Figure 7 Mehdi's one-month studio recording permit (1993)

This document highlights the necessity for musicians, composers, and lyricists to secure an official permit from Ershād to record their audio works in a studio for a specific production. The permit is valid for one month.

Source: National Archives of Iran – Document No: 4657036. (Appendix figure for page 57)

Appendix H

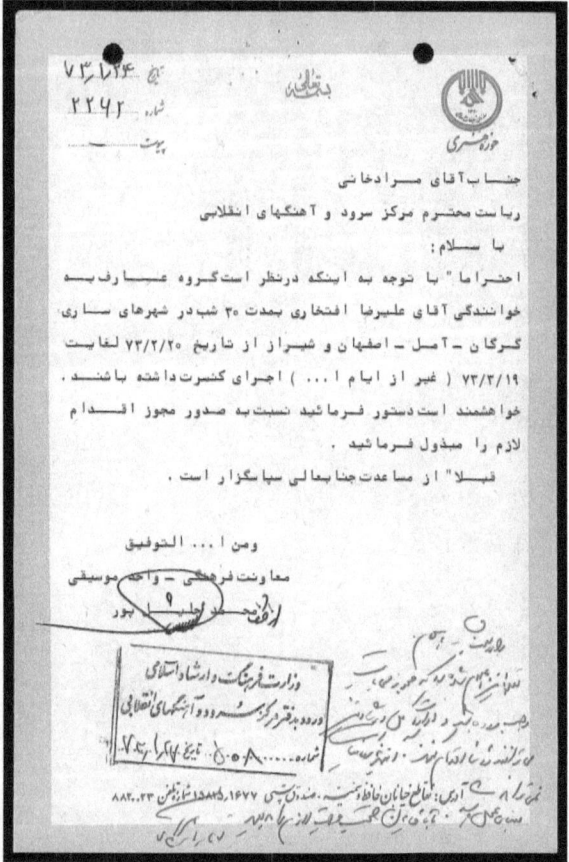

Figure 8 Eftekhari's One-Month Concert Permit Request (1994)[81]

This document is a request made in 1994 by the Music Center at the Artistic Division of the Islamic Revolution to Ershād for a one-month permit for the Aref Ensemble, with Alierza Eftekhari as the singer, to perform concerts in Sari, Gorgan, Amol, Isfahan, and Shiraz.

Source: National Archives of Iran – Document No: 4687284. (Appendix figure for page 57)

---

[81] Ali-Reza Eftekhari (born 1958) is an Iranian traditional and popular music singer.

Appendix I

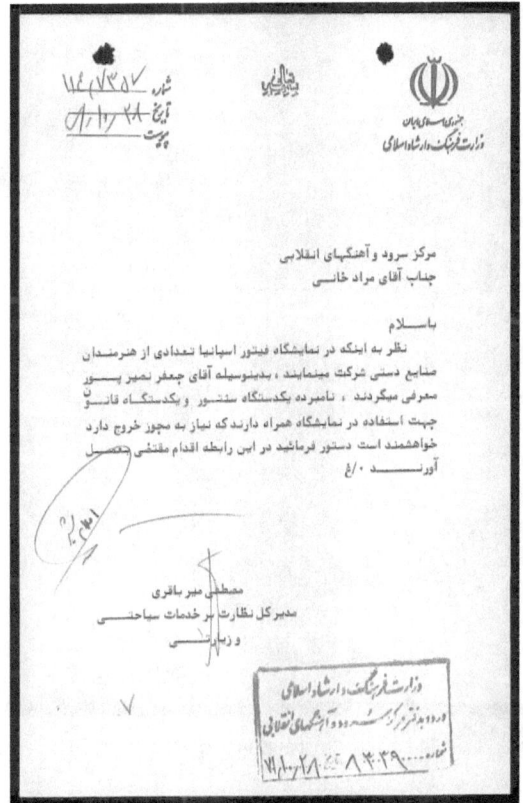

Figure 9 Border Permit Request for Musical Instrument Transportation (1993)

This document, originating from the Director of the Travel and Pilgrimage Services Department at Ershad, requests a border permit for Mr. Nassirpour's musical instruments. The request is addressed to the Sorud and Revolutionar Center of Ershad, indicating Nasirpour's intention to transport the *santur* and *qānun*[82] for the Fitur Art and Craft Fair in Spain.

Source: National Archives of Iran – Document No: 4654529. (Appendix figure for page 57)

---

[82] *Qānun* is a traditional Middle Eastern string instrument, revered for its unique sound.

Appendix J

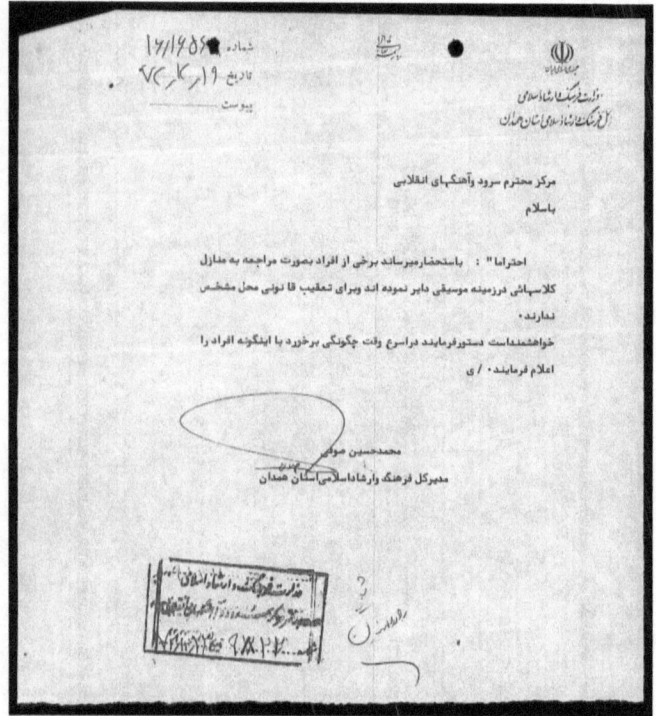

Figure 10 Ershād Letter: Prosecution Procedure for Music Teachers

This document, authored by the director of Ershād-e Hamedān[83] in 1994, is directed towards the Ershād Soroud Centre, highlighting the concern of individuals offering in-home music lessons without a clear address for legal identification. The absence of a fixed location complicates the enforcement of legal measures. The director requests prompt guidance on how to address this issue effectively.

Source: National Archives of Iran – Document No: 4678444. (Appendix figure for page 73)

---

[83] Ershād-e Hamedān: Refers to the provincial branch of the of Ershād organization in Iran, located in Hamedān province.

Appendix K

Figure 11 Chang Institution Operating Permit (1985)

Issued in 1985, this document grants legal permission for the operation of the Chang Institution. It includes a stipulation requesting the institution to regularly submit monthly reports detailing its activities to Ershād.

Source: National Archives of Iran – Document No: 4685029. (Appendix figure for page 76)

Glossary

Ālāt o adavāt-e musiqi: Refers to musical instruments

Artwashing: Refers to the practice of promoting state-approved art to shape public perception and mask controversial or oppressive actions, often by highlighting specific artistic expression while censoring others.

Bābā: A term used in Persian to refer to one's father, often as a term of endearment or respect.

Basiji: Refers to members of the Basij Resistance Force, a volunteer paramilitary organization in Iran. They are known for their loyalty to the Islamic Republic and often assist in various social, political, and military activities.

Bazmi: Denotes the joyful and celebratory ambiance of Persian gatherings characterized by music, poetry, and various cultural activities.

Chādor: A traditional Iranian garment, worn by women, consisting of a large piece of cloth that covers the head and body, leaving only the face visible. After the 1979 Revolution, compulsory hijab was introduced, with black chadors being emphasized by officials.

Chappi: A term referring to leftist or Marxist individuals or groups in Iran. It is often used to describe those who advocate for socialist or communist ideologies and policies.

Dāyere-ye Mobāreze bā Monkarāt: A government-backed ideological organization in Iran tasked with enforcing moral and religious codes.

Ershād: Iran's Ministry of Culture and Islamic Guidance, oversees cultural affairs and media access. It regulates content conflicting with Islamic values to ensure alignment between religion and state laws. Individuals must obtain permits from this ministry to publish books, release music albums, hold concerts, and more.

Faqih: An Islamic jurist who interprets and implements Islamic law based on the Quran and Hadith.

Fatwā: A religious ruling in Islamic law

Goruh-e sorud: Vocal Ensemble, typically consisting of men and boys since female vocal performance was no longer permitted under Islamic law after the 1979 revolution in Iran.

Gozinesh: In Iran, although the investigation of beliefs is explicitly prohibited under Article 23 of the Iranian Constitution, the Gozinesh Law, enacted after the 1979 Revolution, restricts the participation of religious and ethnic minorities in civil life. This law imposes ideological screening, primarily based on adherence to Islam, for employment, education, and other opportunities. A prominent example of ideological screening was the Cultural Revolution (1980–1983), when Iranian academia was closed for more than two years, and more than hundreds of professors and thousands of students were dismissed to purge Western and non-Islamic influences and align with revolutionary and political Islam.

Hāj-Āqā: A Persian term used to respectfully address an elderly man, typically someone who has completed the Hajj pilgrimage to Mecca. In certain contexts, it can also imply a position of authority.

Halāl: Signifies what is permissible in Islamic law

Harām: Refers to what is forbidden in Islamic law

Hawza: An Islamic seminary for religious study

Herāsat: A security and intelligence agency in Iran responsible for maintaining internal security, monitoring government

Glossary

institutions, and ensuring adherence to Islamic principles within organizations.

IRGC: *See* Sepāh

IRIB: *See* Sedā o Simā

Jamaran Hussainia: Located in the north of Tehran, alongside the residence of Ayatollah Khomeini in Jamaran, this was where he delivered his speeches after the revolution.

Khotbeh: Refers to the sermon delivered by an Islamic cleric during Friday prayers, typically addressing religious and social matters within the community.

Komite: Refers to the Islamic Revolution Committees, a militia established by Imam Khomeini after the 1979 Revolution. These committees enforced Islamic law and played a significant role in supporting the regime's policies through arrests and other actions.

Makruh: An Islamic term referring to discouraged or disliked actions, but not explicitly forbidden. These actions are considered less favorable than permissible ones but do not incur sin if performed.

Markaz-e Sorud-e Sedā o Simā: IRIB Music Center

Mojavvez-e Musiqi: Refers to permits required by professional musicians in Iran following the revolution. These permits were necessary for activities such as transporting their musical instruments, as well as recording music and live performances. They are typically issued for a specific duration and limited purposes.

Motreb: The word "motreb" stems from the Arabic verb "taraba," meaning "to make happy." Initially used for all musicians in Iran, "motreb" later became pejoratively associated with entertainers.

Motrebi: "Motrebi" refers to the practice or style associated with "motrebs," entertainers who use music to amuse the audience.

Musiqi: Music

Musiqi-e asil-e Irani: Translates to traditional Persian music, characterized by its unique modal system (*dastgāh*), intricate melodies, and emphasis on improvisation. It is deeply rooted in Iranian culture and history, reflecting the country's diverse regional influences and artistic heritage.

Musiqi-e mobtazal: Translates to "vulgar" or "decadent music" in English. It is often used after the 1979 revolution in Iran to describe Motrebi music.

Musiqi-e zir-zamini: Translates to "underground music" in English. It refers to youth creating popular music in Iran, including rock and hip-hop, without reliance on permits from Ershād.

NIRT: *See* Radio o Televizion-e Melli-e Iran

Orf: Refers to customary practices or traditions observed within a community or society, particularly those that are not explicitly defined by religious or legal authorities but are widely accepted and followed.

Pahlavis: Refers to the ruling dynasty of Iran from 1925 to 1979, headed by Reza Shah Pahlavi and later by his son, Mohammad Reza Shah Pahlavi.

Pāsdār (Sepāhi): A term used in Iran to refer to a member of the Sepāh, translating to "Guardian" or "Guard."

Radio o Televizion-e Melli-e Iran: Before the 1979 Revolution, "NIRT" stood for National Iranian Radio and Television.

Glossary

Sāzmān-e Tabliqāt-e Islāmi: The Islamic Development Organization is an Iranian religious and cultural organization founded under the order of Imam Khomeini after the 1979 Revolution. It promotes the ideologies of the Islamic Republic under the supervision of the Supreme Leader.

Sedā o Simā: After the revolution, NIRT was reorganized and became Islamic Republic of Iran Broadcasting (IRIB).

Sepāh: Sepāh, short for Sepāh-e Pāsdārān-e Enqelāb-e Eslāmi, is the Islamic Revolutionary Guard Corps of Iran. It was established after the 1979 Revolution to protect the country's Islamic system and ideals and is tasked with safeguarding the political system of the Islamic Republic of Iran. The IRGC has a significant role in Iran's military, political, and economic spheres, operating independently from the regular armed forces.

Shāh: A Persian term for "king." The last Shah of Iran, Mohammad Reza Pahlavi, commonly known as the Shah, ruled from 1941 until the 1979 revolution.

Sharia: The moral and legal framework of Islam, derived from the Quran, Hadith, and other Islamic texts, governing aspects of daily life and religious practices.

Sorud: Initially meaning "anthem," was repurposed by the Islamic Republic of Iran authorities who substituted the term "music" (musiqi) with "sorud," for their propaganda agenda after the revolution. This semantic shift allowed them to utilize musical expression for their own objectives while avoiding the term "music."

TSO: The Tehran Symphony Orchestra (TSO), based in Tehran and founded in 1933, is Iran's most prestigious symphony orchestra. Following the 1979 Revolution, many musicians emigrated to Europe and the US. For the next decade, the TSO had reduced activity, with performances mainly held for officials and at revolutionary ceremonies.

References

Breyley, G. J. (2016). Between the Cracks: Street Music in Iran. *Journal of Musicological Research, 35*(2), 72–81. https://doi.org/10.1080/01411896.2016.1165051

Breyley, G. J., & Fatemi, S. (2016). *Iranian music and popular entertainment from Motrebi to Losanjelesi and beyond.* Routledge.

Creswell, J. W. (2012). *Educational Research: Planning, Conducting, and Evaluating Quantitative and Qualitative Research, Enhanced Pearson eText with Loose-Leaf Version—Access Card Package. Pearson Education, Inc.*

Ghazi, F. (2019). *Dādgāh-e Mohammad-Ali Najafi* [Trial of Mohammad-Ali Najafi]. Article in Persian. *BBC Persian.* Retrieved March 12, 2020 from https://www.bbc.com/persian/iran-features-49034915

Hamedani, A. (Director). (2017). *Tavallod-e Yek Talar* [The Birth of a Hall, Story of Birth of Tehran Roudaki Hall; Documentary film]. BBC Persian. https://www.youtube.com/watch?v=Z5jVVGqHLxc

Hemmasi, F. (2020). *Duke University Press—Tehrangeles Dreaming.* https://www.dukeupress.edu/tehrangeles-dreaming

Hosseini, S. V. (Director). (2016). *Bazm-e Razm* [Drums of War; Documentary film]. Revayat-e Fath.

"Javāb-e moštarak-e Seda o Sima,." (2018). *Javāb-e moštarak-e Sedā o Simā be šekāyat-e Shajarian va xānevādey-e Farhad* [The response of IRIB to lawsuits of Shajarian and Farhad's family]. Article in Persian. *Iran Online.* Retrieved March 1, 2020 from http://www.ion.ir/news/409586/شکایت-شجریان-از-صدا-و-سیما

Kamali Dehghan, S. (2014). Iran Broadcaster Breaks Rule Over Musical Instruments Played on TV. *The Guardian.* Retrieved February 18, 2020 from https://www.theguardian.com/world/2014/jan/22/iran-broadcaster-rule-musical-instruments-tv

References

Kifner, J. (1979, July 24). Khomeini Bans Broadcast Music, Saying It Corrupts Iranian Youth. https://www.nytimes.com/1979/07/24/archives/khomeini-bans-broadcast-music-saying-it-corrupts-iranian-youth.html

Keshtkar, O. (2016, September 7). *Arash veleś nakon – album-e tāzey -e Kiosk* [Kiosk's New Album – Arash, Don't leave it off]. Article in Persian. *Radio Zamaneh*. Retrieved March 22, 2020 from https://www.radiozamaneh.com/297748

Kojuri, N. (2018). *Sanad-e tārixi-e esteftā az mahzar-e Imam Khomeini darbāreye musiqi* [The document of requesting a fatwā about music from Ayatollah Khomeini]. Article in Persian. *Imam Khomeini*. Retrieved March 3, 2020 from http://www.imam-khomeini.ir/fa/the-document-of-requesting-a-fatwā-about-music-from-Ayatollah-Khomeini

Mohseni, A. (Director). (2005). *Zendegi* [Life; Documentary film]. Kelk-e Khial. https://Y2u.be/ZdYxrujW3RM

Mojaver, F. (2009). Sources of economic growth and stagnation in Iran. *The Journal of International Trade & Economic Development*, *18*(2), 275–295. https://doi.org/10.1080/09638190902916519

Niknafs, N. (2016). In a box: a narrative of a/n (under)grounded Iranian musician. *Music Education Research*, *18*(4), 351–363. https://doi.org/10.1080/14613808.2016.1202222

Nooshin, L. (2005). Underground, Overground: Rock Music and Youth Discourses in Iran. *Iranian Studies*, *38*(3), 463–494. JSTOR.

Nooshin, L. (2017). Whose liberation? Iranian popular music and the fetishization of resistance. *Popular Communication*, *15*(3), 163–191. https://doi.org/10.1080/15405702.2017.1328601

Pear, R., & Times, S. T. the N. Y. (1988, July 21). Khomeini Accepts 'Poison' of Ending the War with Iraq; U.N. Sending Mission. *The New York Times*. Retrieved February 2, 2020 from https://www.nytimes.com/1988/07/21/us/khomeini-accepts-poison-of-ending-the-war-with-iraq-un-sending-mission.html

Rahimi, B. (2015). Censorship and the Islamic Republic: Two Modes of Regulatory Measures for Media in Iran. *Middle East Journal, 69*(3), 358–378. JSTOR.

Rahimi, T. (2017a). *Sorud-e Khomeini ey Imam do sāl mamnu bud* [Khomeini Ey Imam was banned for two years]. Article in Persian. *Tārix-e Irani.* Retrieved March 22, 2020 from http://tarikhirani.ir/fa/news/Khomeini-Ey-Imam-was-banned-for-two-years

Rahimi, T. (2017b). *Navārhāyemān rā basāt mikardim va miforuxtim* [We sold our music cassettes as street vendors]. Article in Persian. *Tārix-e Irani.* Retrieved March 22, 2020 from http://tarikhirani.ir/fa/news/we-sold-our-music-cassettes-as-street-vendors

Randall, A. J. (2004). *Music, Power, and Politics.* Routledge.

Razi, P. (2016, August 22). *Kiosk bā nohomin album; Stereo Tull az rāh miresad* [Kiosk's ninth album, "Stereo Tull Presents"]. Article in Persian. *Radio Farda.* Retrieved March 22, 2020 from https://www.radiofarda.com/a/f35-kiosk-9th-album/27937275.html

Refugees, U. N. H. C. for. (2001). *Refworld | Child Soldiers Global Report 2001—Iran.* Refworld. https://www.refworld.org/docid/498805f02d.html

"Ruzi ke paxš-e musiqi az radio va televizion qad-e qan shod." (2019). *Ruzi ke paxš-e musiqi az radio o televizion qad-e qan shod* [The day that broadcasting music was banned at IRIB]. Article in Persian. *Rouydad24.* Retrieved March 21, 2020 from https://www.rouydad24.ir/fa/news/the-day-that-broadcasting-music-was-banned-at-IRIB

Seidman, I. (2006). *Interviewing as qualitative research: A guide for researchers in education and the social sciences* (3rd ed). Teachers College Press.

Semati, M. (2017). Sounds like Iran: On popular music of Iran. *Popular Communication, 15*(3), 155–162. https://doi.org/10.1080/15405702.2017.1343609

Seyedsayamdost, N. (2017). *Soundtrack of the revolution: The politics of music in Iran*. Stanford University Press.

Shahshahani, S. (2013). The Sounds of Music in Tehran. *Anthropology of the Middle East; Oxford, 8*(1), 24–39.

http://dx.doi.org.myaccess.library.utoronto.ca/10.3167/ame.2013.080103

"Some singers do not,." (2013). *Barxi xānandehā bexāter-e xārej az arześhā nemiguyand* [Some singers are not speaking of [Islamic Republic of Iran's] values not to lose any of their audience in their concerts abroad]. Article in Persian. *TasnimNews*. Retrieved April 1, 2020 from https://www.tasnimnews.com/news/some-singers-are-not-speaking-of-values

Tasnim News Agency. (2019, February 10). *40 Sāl 40 Ālbum: Negāhi be album-e Shrangiz; nakhostin konsert-e Jomhuri-ye Eslami bā sedāye Nazeri, Kamkar va Tarif*. Tasnim News Agency. https://www.tasnimnews.com/fa/news/1397/11/21/1943747/40

Tyler, P. E. (1988, March 22). *Damage by Iraqi Missiles Evident In Tehran*. Washington Post.
https://www.washingtonpost.com/archive/politics/1988/03/22/damage-by-iraqi-missiles-evident-in-tehran/379d1850-67c9-4f0c-b19c-ca4a1dbf1846/

Youssefzadeh, A. (2000). The situation of music in Iran since the Revolution: The role of official organizations. *British Journal of Ethnomusicology, 9*(2), 35–61.
https://doi.org/10.1080/09681220008567300

Asemana Books is devoted to publishing diasporic, underrepresented, and progressive literature on the Middle East.

asemanabooks.ca

ASEMANA
BOOKS

www.ingramcontent.com/pod-product-compliance
Lightning Source LLC
Chambersburg PA
CBHW020420230426
43663CB00007BA/1252